DABAN

On Modifying

KURDISH

Language

By Means Of Unification

Hussein Qutbi

First Edition (Revised)

Publication Date 18 Jul. 2024

ISBN 978-1-7391008-2-7

Ebook ISBN 978-1-7391008-3-4

Copyright © 2024 Hussein Qutbi

All rights reserved. No part of this publication may be reproduced, distributed, or transmitted in any form or by any means, including photocopying, recording, or other electronic or mechanical methods, without the prior written permission of the publisher, except in the case of brief quotations embodied in critical reviews and certain other noncommercial uses permitted by copyright law. For permission requests, write to the publisher, addressed "Attention: Permissions Coordinator," at on.modifying.Kurdish@gmail.com

To all who have shaped my identity and contributed to making me who I am..

Contents

Introduction 9

I. Overview 13
    1.1 Status 13
    1.2 Modification 17

II. Development of Languages 21
    2.1 Diachronic Updates 23
    2.2 Linguistic Instability 29
    2.3 Linguistic Interference 35
    2.4 Logical Structure 39

III. Evolution of Kurdish 43
    3.1 Roots 43
    3.2 The Pahlavi 46
    3.3 Colloquial Kurdish 47
    3.4 Future of Kurdish 53
    3.5 Modification of Kurdish 56

IV. A Language Is a Nation 61
    4.1 Nationalism 63
    4.2 Language & Nationalism 67
    4.3 Bilingualism 69
    4.4 Constitutional Recognition 73
    4.5 Role of Religion 80
    4.6 Evolution of Sub-Nations 84

V. Language Ideology 87

5.1 Stratum (Language Prestige) 89
5.2 Language Planning 92
5.3 Language Policy 96

VI. Phonology & Orthography 105
6.1 Phonetics & Phonology 106
6.2 Writing systems 110

VII. Language Segregation 119
7.1 Linguistic Barriers 120
7.2 Sub-Ethnic Fragments 123

IIX. Kurdish Language Strategy 131
8.1 Struggle for Identity 132
8.2 Practical Solutions 136

IX. Diglossia & Digraphia 167
9.1 Diglossia 168
9.2 Orthography 173
9.3 Phonology 183
9.4 Grammar 186
9.5 Semantics 189

X. Unification 191
10.1 Scope of Unification 192
10.2 Why Unification 194
10.3 Examples of Unification 201

Bibliography 213

Preface

For some, like myself, a word can joyfully play with meanings; it can perform elegantly in a sentence, akin to a dancer moving gracefully on stage, connoting ambiguous essence, while grammar serves as a dissonance-reducing music that harmonizes the dancer's movements. For others, including some dear friends, a word is a long-awaited target to capture; language is a battleground permeated with the smell of gunpowder, reminiscent of the struggles in the mountainous regions during the 1980s, where the conflict prominently centered around linguistic recognition.

This book is a discourse on both the beauty and the power of words, without aiming to propose a specific linguistic model. Language formation necessitates a collective effort involving linguists, historians, economists, international relations experts, scholars, and politicians working together in a coordinated and cooperative manner. Understanding the need for comprehensive comprehension before undertaking a project as significant as Kurdish unification helps avoid the mistakes made at the beginning of the twentieth century when Kurdish was formally divided into two sublanguages.

This book also highlights sociolinguistics and political repercussions, treating the issue as a geopolitical linguistic challenge rather than merely a phonological or lexicological study. It calls for rethinking and reforming the Kurdish language, which seems to be sinking into the contemporary global cultural milieu and represents an ambitious attempt to explore those geopolitical dimensions. I extend my gratitude to all my friends who helped bring this book to light and to those who carried the message forward, implementing the idea.

Introduction

For a long time, the world recognized the Kurds as a group of tribes rather than a cohesive nation capable of establishing and sustaining a state with institutions governed by recognized international contexts, systems, relations, and agreements. This perception was so entrenched that the victorious powers of World War I, particularly the British and French, were not convinced of the Kurds' ability to establish and maintain an independent and unified political framework, capable be integrated into their broader project of constructing a new Middle East—a project meticulously designed to safeguard their interests and ensure the smooth implementation of their future agendas and strategies. Consequently, the social fragmentation and the underdeveloped Kurdish nationalist sentiments, as a contemporary political project, were among the most significant reasons for the failures that marked this critical period in modern Kurdish history. This perspective led those concerned to seek solutions exclusively within political frameworks, without paying sufficient attention to the social roots or investigating the negative effects of sociolinguistic fragmentation.

Language, on the other hand, in any nation, is one of the most critical bonds that unify its components, fostering cohesion among regions and solidifying national unity. The neglect that the Kurdish language has endured, and the deprivation of opportunities for it to evolve in line with social changes, have significantly hindered its natural growth. This neglect, manifested in the failure to develop a unified classical language played a vigorous role in the social fissure.

Until a century ago, Kurdish was primarily confined to oral communication, which reinforced linguistic division and accelerated the divergence of dialects, leading to a decline in mutual intelligibility. As a result, the language could not fully play its historical role in advancing the Kurdish national project or in establishing a collective identity that could serve as a solid foundation for a political national entity. This linguistic fragmentation also contributed to the lack of widespread nationalist sentiments as a modern national project, capable of mobilization toward building a modern Kurdish identity.

However, the circumstances at the threshold of the twenty-first century, particularly following two significant events that politically, culturally, and socially shook the Middle East, allowed for revolutionary linguistic changes in Kurdish. These changes included the formulation of writing systems, providing it with a historic opportunity for development. The two events were the outbreak of World War I and the October Revolution, which led to the fall of the two largest empires in the region—the Russian in 1917 and the Ottoman in 1924.

Despite the severe fragmentation in Kurdish society, both in its tribal fabric and linguistic composition, most political analysts at the time attributed the failures to purely political factors, neglecting to consider other possibly more critical causes, such as the sociolinguistic fragmentation that clearly illustrates the weakness of the Kurdish language. This weakness, particularly the absence of a unified classical dialect, was a significant reason for the stagnation of the comprehensive Kurdish national project, which was supposed to rally the Kurdish regions and strengthen nationalist sentiments, similar to what occurred during the Great Arab Revolution.

This book discusses the pros and cons of unifying the Kurdish language without delving into specific methodologies or favoring particular linguistic laws or writing systems. Instead, it emphasizes the importance of developing the language to keep pace with social, scientific, and political changes and the role this plays in shaping a modern Kurdish society. The chapters of the book cover the fundamentals of language in general, the mutual influence between language and social lifestyles, and the outcomes that the project of unifying the classical Kurdish language could provide—not only for Kurdish as a language but also, importantly, for the Kurds as a nation. Whenever the term "Kurdistan" is used in this book, it refers to all the cohesive geographical areas where Kurdish speakers, or those of Kurdish national origin, constitute the majority. The term "Kurdish" refers to the sum of dialects and linguistic variations that collectively form the Kurdish language.

Hussein Qutbi

London 2024

Abbreviations

The East	Eastern part of the Kurdish landscape (Western Iran).
The North	The northern part of the Kurdish landscape (Eastern Turkey).
Roj.	Rojava (Kurdish landscape of North Syria).
The South	The Kurdish-speaking region in Iraq
KRG	Kurdish Regional Government of Iraqi-Kurdistan
Eng.	In English
Kurm.	In Kurmanji dialect
Sor.	In Sorani dialect

I. Overview

"Die Grenzen meiner Sprache sind die Grenzen meiner Welt. (The limits of my language mean the limits of my world.)"

Wittgenstein, 1922

Kurdish is the name given to a group of varieties that are emotionally bonded together, yet known for the low level of mutual intelligibility more than denoting an integrated language according to the linguistic definition of the term 'Language'.

1.1 Status

In general, the Kurdish language is not unique in dialectal diversity since low intelligibility is observed in many living languages worldwide. Varieties of Italian, German, and Arabic are examples of low comprehensibility; except that each of these languages has managed to stitch the dialects through a common formal standard while Kurdish has still not achieved this stage of development. Thus, this language requires an ultimate modification, particularly coining a unique formal variety to be used as a cross-dialectal umbrella.

A consenteneous well-designed standard provides, in addition to linguistic unity, the groundwork to achieve two main goals: the first is to come up with a **modern linguistic domain** that is capable of handling academic advancement (measured by precision in transferring thoughts and concepts), and the second is to augment the national and **sociocultural unity** taking into account the capability of the language to influence social norms.

Conspicuously, Kurdish for the Kurds resembles water for fish; the cleaner it gets, the more they can comprehend each other.

1.1.1 A Language or a Group of Sub-Languages?

As the borderline between what is a dialect and what is a language is so thin and ambiguous that in some cases it is confusing, it may not be so difficult for one to deem a certain variety as a dialect of another, and at the same time, it is not hard for others to regard that certain variety as a separate, independent, full-fledged language. Any of the main four Kurdish dialects (**Kurmanji**, **Sorani**, **Zaza**-Dimli/Gorani, and **Pahlawani**/Luri) may be considered a separate language by non-Kurdish authorities and even by some linguists; the Zaza (Gorani), for instance, despite being defined by the speaker population as a dialect of Kurdish, the Turkish authority classifies it as a separate language. Also, according to German scholar Terry Lynn Todd (2008, p. vi), the Dimly–Zaza is not a Kurdish dialect but rather a separate West Iranian language. The same could be applied to Pahlawani, Kurmanji, and Sorani.

Comparing the language of education in the Iraqi-Kurdistan region with its counterpart in Rojava, it resembles two discrete languages with different alphabets, vocabulary, and syntax rules. Furthermore, subdialects are growing fast such as the Pahlawani groups, Luri, Laki, and Kalhuri.

1.1.2 Political Repercussions

The absence of a unified form of language was one of the main reasons that reflected an inaccurate image of the Kurds, manifesting the nation not as a distinct integrated but rather as internally isolated tribes who may easily accept division and consent to breaking their homeland over the neighboring states. Not only the external vision but also the internal sense of identity is affected by this gloomy outlook, accepting and prioritizing the sub-ethnic identities as solid facts. The linguistic segregation signified the notion of ethnic disintegration, planted the thought of divisions in the minds of the Kurds, and spread the introversive attitude; thus, in the twentieth century, when time and circumstances allowed the British and the French to establish the current independent countries, the concept of Kurdishness failed to enforce an atmosphere of independent state. Moreover, when the time came for coining a modern grammar, instead of seizing the opportunity for persisting ethnic unity by a unified linguistic standard, the language was already reshaped in a dual form, separating the two major dialects, Kurmanji and Sorani, leaving, the same time, other dialects outclassed with no will or interest shown in. This act of splitting the linguistic identity has in turn deepened the gap further; resulting in more isolation and disintegration to the extent that today has reached an alarming level of endangering the unity of the ethnic composition.

If the administrations and intellectual communities continue to ignore the linguistic dynamic evolution, each dialect would consider separation as a full-fledged language, and this would inevitably affect ethnic integrity. Taking into consideration how dialects blossom into independent languages, a rational futuristic view shows that "Kurdish" is in danger of disintegrating, similar to Latin and Pahlavi, and the word "Kurds" as a nation with no unique living language is associated with ancient groups such as Slavic and Iranic.

1.1.3 Previous Studies

Historically, Kurdish has been subject to noticeable neglect, however, in recent centuries it has received a share of the essential studies and research. Ernest N. McCarus (1958) lists the pioneering works on Kurdish, stating that they date back at least to the Italian linguist and missionary P. Maurizio Garzoni (1734-1804), who published *"Grammatica e vocabolario dea ingua Kurda"* in Rome in 1787. The book consists of a 79-page grammatical sketch in addition to other 200 pages of vocabulary collected in the town of Amadiya and spelled in terms of Italian orthography. The Russian linguist

Alexander Chodzko (1804–1891) published his 60-page grammatical sketch, *Etudes philologiques sur la langue kurde*, in Paris in 1857, based on the dialect of Sulaimania with a French transcription and Persian script for citations. The other Russian (German-born) Peter Ivanovich Lerch published his two-part book *Forschungen Über Die Kurden Und Die Iranischen Nordchaldäer*, in German 1857–58. The first part contained Kurmanji and Zaza texts obtained from Kurdish prisoners of war in Smolensk, and the second consisted of an introduction and a 30-page Kurdish-German glossary. In 1880, the other German Ferdinand Justi (1837–1907) produced a comparative study on phonology and morphology, *Kurdische Grammatik*. The Kurdish also attracted the British Samuel A. Rhea published *Brief Grammar and Vocabulary of the Kurdish Language of the Hakari District*, (1869).

The Western interest continued in the twentieth century through the propagation of the Swiss Albert Socin's *Die Sprache der Kurden*, 1898; the French J. de Morgan, *Études Linguistiques: Dialectes Kurdes*, 1904; the German Oskar Mann, *Die Mundart der Mukri-Kurden*, 1906; the valuable British E. B. Soane, *Elementary Kurmanji Grammar*, 1913. (based on the Sulaimaniya dialect); and the French Abbe Paul Beidar, *Grammaire kurde*, 1926. (McCarus E, 1958, p. 3).

1.1.4 Modernization Attempt

The actual modernization of Kurdish only began in the early 20th century with desperate attempts to create practical writing systems. However, considering the circumstances hitherto, many important linguistic aspects were absent, neglected, or poorly prioritized. Just as beginnings are always hasty, those first steps suffered from a trickle yet effectual shortcomings, the most notable of which is the geographical (local) scope of resources, the unawareness of the sociolinguistic role in building a unified nation, and the phonological trends manifested in the exaggerated stress on phonetics at the expense of spelling flexibility.

In more detail, the linguistic resources considered for vocabulary were focused narrowly on dialectal scope instead of the comprehensive language entirety, which consequently imposed a

I. Overview

regional limit on the deployment and usage of the formal standards, i.e., looking the vocabulary up either in Sorani or Kurmanji without considering the common roots and resources of both varieties.

In addition to the geographical limitations, major attention was given to phonetics rather than transcription. This is significantly remarked in standardizing Sorani, where the main attention was focused on the details of the sound of the letter (<u>phoneme</u>), distinguishing the different shades of the phoneme (<u>allophones</u>) by different graphemes (letters), for example, using a diacritic sign to separate the dark from the light 'L' (ڵ /ɫ/ and ل /l/), 'R' (ڕ and ر), and 'Y' (ی /ɪ/ and ێ /ɪə/). The negative impact of this approach is that the sound of a word may differ from one village to the next, and in the same village from time to time, while in contrast, the more flexible and inclusive written shape of a vocabulary can rise above all pronunciations, allowing a wider range of accents and dialects to understand and communicate comprehensively.

At the start of the twenty-first century, the Kurdish, in light of scientific advancement and sociocultural alteration, is imperatively required to start the second step of modification.

1.2 Modification

Dynamic evolution imposes constant linguistic changes on every language around the world (Steels & Szathmáry, 2018, par. 1), necessitating ongoing modification; consequently, it is common for human languages to struggle with updates and modifications. For example, despite its solid status as the most globally popular language, English endures noticeable dialectal inconsistencies between conservative British and radical American variants. This divergence transpired when the linguist Noah Webster (1758–1843) institutionalized *Standard American English* (SAE) by publishing the American Spelling Book in 1783. Conversely, linguistic variation may also impact cultural harmony; Chinese multi-dialectal unintelligibility has left China in a relentless quest for a common national language since the end of the First Opium War in 1842. Gina Anne Tam (2020, p. 35) highlights that linguistic disharmony played a central role in China's defeat in that war:

> *"[The defeat was] forcing many elites to wonder if their problem was much more foundational – that their weakness lay not in something concrete like infrastructure, but rather, the country's very cultural anatomy, of which language was a central part."*

To address the issue of dialectal intelligibility, many languages worldwide have established formal standards by selecting one of the existing dialects. This selection is often influenced by political or economic preferences and is enforced by a powerful national authority. Examples include the selection of Tuscan for Italian, Tagalog for Filipino, and Parisian for French. However, some languages, like Norwegian, continue to struggle with the issue of dual formal dialects, Bokmål and Nynorsk. Generally, there is a wealth of accumulated experience globally that could benefit the Kurdish language as it considers linguistic enhancement.

Also, geopolitical developments underscore the importance of linguistic modification in strengthening a nation's stance. Unity becomes increasingly crucial as political forecasts predict intense global competition for resources, leaving little room for socially disintegrated minorities. Powerful nations with firm social structures will survive, while smaller ones risk dissolution into larger neighbors if they do not form protective regional unions based on politics, economy, and cultural relationships. To avoid a challenging struggle for survival in the future, scholars and linguists must act swiftly at this developmental stage to promote linguistic modification. This involves building bridges for internal unity and using cultural relationships to approximate interests with neighboring nations.

If efforts were made to increase mutual intelligibility among the dispersed Kurdish-speaking populace, the outcome would be immensely beneficial for unifying the nation. This unity would reflect economic advancement, political power, and social cohesion. In other words, the survival of the Kurdish nation in the coming centuries heavily relies on its ability to develop a unified language that can form the basis of a powerful nation, capable of protecting its position

I. Overview

among intrusive neighbors. To conclude, long-standing prosperity cannot be achieved without social unity or, more importantly, without a common formal dialect to serve as an internal communication tool.

1.2.1 The Second Phase

The positive steps taken by Wahbi and Bedirxan, the founders of the modern Kurdish orthographies, at the beginning of the 20th century, transformed Kurdish from diverse, unwritten tribal varieties into an orthographically capable language suitable for modern official and academic use. However, their efforts encountered significant limitations, such as the lack of a well-developed language plan, the absence of an authoritative body to implement language policy, scarce linguistic and philological resources, and logistical challenges in collecting sufficient data from the vast array of Kurdish dialects. These limitations, given the advancements and tools available today, are no longer insurmountable. The present moment is ripe for initiating a new chapter in the Kurdish cultural and linguistic revolution.

A diverse language like Kurdish, spoken by tens of millions with low inter-dialect intelligibility and no centralized power, should be modified to adopt flexible syntactical and orthographic rules. This flexibility would allow the inclusion of a broad range of speakers, allowing as many varieties as possible to reach as much familiarity as possible. However, the current strict orthographic systems do not efficiently accommodate this diversity. For instance, Sorani spellings were based on the pronunciation of colloquial words from a limited region (Sulaymaniyah). In contrast, the orthography of a diverse language like Kurdish should consider the pronunciations and grammatical rules across a much larger area, if not all accents and dialects.

Since the emergence of two semi-independent Kurdish administrative entities, the Kurdistan Regional Government (KRG) and, to some extent, in Northern Syria, the feasibility of implementing a language policy has become a reality for the first time in modern history. Additionally, the widespread use of social media has provided a robust foundation for disseminating an advanced form of the language quickly, widely, and cost-effectively. Therefore, laying the groundwork for the second phase of Kurdish language modernization is not only possible but urgent.

The shortcomings of the Wahbi-Bedirxan initiative, viewed as the initial phase of Kurdish modernization, necessitate a completion step better characterized as the second phase. Given the qualitative transformations in social and political contexts over the past century, this second phase is now more crucial and urgent to ensure the language can adapt to contemporary updates and needs.

1.2.2 Limitations

Despite the consensus on the importance of unifying classical Kurdish, a careful observer may notice some conflicting emotions; some individuals approach the idea with ambition, while others are apprehensive. Proponents recognize the necessity of such an extensive academic endeavor and advocate for the establishment of a strong and cohesive nation based on cultural and linguistic unity, which could enhance economic, social, and political capacities. Conversely, skeptics fear the potential elimination of certain vernaculars or the dominance of specific dialects over others. Among scholars, some express concern about the uncertain fate of their literary works if the current linguistic form is abandoned. The most frequent objection arises from a misunderstanding that the proposed formal academic dialect is intended to replace vernacular usage in daily life. In reality, unification is meant primarily for formal education and administrative purposes, focusing on written communication rather than spoken language.

Overall, in the contemporary Kurdish mindset, political ambitions seem to overshadow cultural demands and concerns. There is no doubt that the long history of tragic events experienced by the Kurds in modern times has cast a shadow over the collective mindset, creating a sense of fear and an urgent desire for immediate practical solutions rather than rational long-term planning. Consequently, a linguistic project is not currently a top priority, and most intellectuals are investing their efforts in political endeavors rather than in developing long-term socio-cultural strategies.

II. Development of Languages

> "People of the twenty-first century are developing new technologies that have already altered the foundations of learning, teaching, art, science, politics, government, business, music, and literature. The most interesting aspect of these exciting innovations is that they are all made possible by a single tool, human language, instrumentum linguae."
>
> Daniel Everett 2012

We may be fascinated by birds singing in the trees ahead of Nowruz, but they may not be celebrating the imminent approach of this ancient festival as we imagine. Instead, birds use their songs primarily to attract mates for the long-awaited process of mating. Additionally, they use sounds to defend their nests against intruders, call their chicks, warn the flock about predators, and even argue with other members of their species that may obtrude on their nests.

Thus, birdsong is a form of communication rather than a joyful celebration. Considering that communication requires a sufficient tool to facilitate the transfer of thoughts, known as "language," the question arises: "Can the sounds of these communicating birds be called a language?" The answer contributes to defining the essence of the term "language." It raises the question of whether language is any form of communication tools, such as signals, signs, and body language, or if it is a more complex system governed by a set of grammatical rules and logical denotations.

Undoubtedly, the term 'language,' with regard to thought complexity, encompasses a wide range of communication skills. This range spans from the most preliminary, like bird vocalizations, to the more complex expressions of human beings, and extends to the most precise machine programming languages, such as Visual Basic and C++ which are fundamentally structured on the principle of maximum precision within a true or false dichotomy.

A human can express simple orders through hand signs and emotions using facial expressions, but advanced demands require a much more powerful tool to convey them. Communicating more complex ideas is akin to transporting a heavier load, as heavy loads need stronger vehicles, advanced thoughts involve more advanced linguistic rules. This fact explains why human languages vary in the complexity of grammatical rules and the depth of lexical entries; it depends mainly on the accuracy of thought transmission.

Although anthropologists do not agree on the origin of human languages, the most popular hypothesis suggests that the initial attempts to create and develop languages began among humans' primate ancestors. These efforts evolved from pre-linguistic systems, such as preliminary indexing and simple vocal expressions, long before Homo sapiens existed. However, according to J. Nicholas (1998), the time required to achieve the current spread and diversity of modern vocal languages is estimated to have started at least 100,000 years ago.

Natural barriers such as rough topography and harsh environmental conditions hinder transportation and communication among groups of language speakers. Isolated groups develop unique sound patterns over time. Additionally, in response to the emergence of complex thoughts and the need to adapt to an ever-changing lifestyle, there has been a continual effort to modify linguistic tools and invent more sophisticated rules. Thus, isolated groups develop their own accents, dialects, ethnolects, and practical languages. While homogeneous flatlands allow for easier transportation, mountainous regions exacerbate communication difficulties among population groups, leading to greater dissimilarity and the evolution of new and distinct language varieties. This fact may explain the abundance of dialects in Kurdish, as the majority of its speakers live in rugged mountainous areas, compared to languages spoken in plains and deserts.

A glance at the world's map of languages reveals that languages historically prevailing in larger areas are associated with warm weather and homogeneous topography that allows for easier

II. Development of Languages

transportation, such as deserts. In contrast, linguistic variation is more prevalent in mountainous, forested, and snowy regions. Over time, the isolation of groups widens the linguistic gap and diminishes mutual understanding. Consequently, mutual intelligibility is the criterion used to determine whether a certain variety is a dialect or an independent language. If a significant shift occurs in a dialect and mutual intelligibility drops below the required level, the mature dialect is considered a new language in its own right.

2.1 Diachronic Updates

The evolution of a language over time reveals significant modifications in its sound system, such as shifts in the sound of the letters (phonemes) or the adoption of near shade of the sound (allophones). Consequently, the pronunciation of a language may differ substantially from that of several centuries earlier. Additionally, changes occur in vocabulary, grammar, and spelling. These phonetic and grammatical variations arise from several factors, including distinct habits used by individuals, among other various environmental and social influences.

2.1.1 Sound Changes

On the individual level, each person possesses a unique vocal tract and auditory cortex, resulting in distinct pronunciation, and the manner of speaking is influenced by pitch, intonation, rhythm, and syllabic stress. This individualized mode of speech is termed an idiolect, characterized by a person's preferred vocabulary and grammatical structures. Collectively, these individual idiolects form dialects, shaped by factors such as social status and educational level.

Phonemes are produced and vary based on airflow constriction in the vocal tract, nasalization, and the positioning and shaping of the tongue. For instance, raising the tongue closer to the roof of the mouth results in a higher phoneme, as exemplified by /ɫ/ in the word 'Mał' (/maɫ/, Sor. 'ماڵ' – Eng. 'home'). This is distinguished in Sorani orthography by a caron over the letter L (Sor. 'ڵ'). Conversely, lowering the tongue produces a lighter 'L' /l/ ('ل'), as seen in the word 'Mil' (/'mɪl/, Sor. 'مل' – Eng. 'neck'). The word 'بەڵێ' (/beɫɪə/, Eng. 'yes') may be pronounced as /belj/ when the tongue is lowered. These variations result from individual speech habits, leading to new sound patterns that may prevail within a community, causing ongoing phonological changes.

Variations occur at almost all core linguistic levels: phonetics, phonology, morphology, syntax, semantics, and more. As Ramzi Naji et al. (2020) note:

> "The most extensively investigated topic in studies of language variation and change, in particular, and in linguistics in general is sound change (henceforth SC). SC is seen as a developmental process pertinent to both phonetics and phonology."

Phonetic bias in Kurdish is evident due to phenomena such as assimilation, elision, and the intrusion of phonemes. These phonetic modifications, detailed in Section 2.1.2, facilitate articulatory ease by simplifying sound production, particularly when it involves blocking airflow, as with non-initial plosive sounds like /d/ and /b/, and the nasal /m/. This adjustment allows for easier passage of air through the vocal tract, resulting in high sound volume with minimal pressure on the lung, which is particularly advantageous in rural and mountainous environments. Consequently, these permanently altered phonemes generate words that differ phonetically from their morphological roots.

2.1.2 Accents

When a group of speakers becomes isolated from others of the same language for an extended period, variations in individual idiolects lead to shifts in pronunciation, resulting in a distinctive manner of speech. These shifts, along with changes in intonation and syllabic stress, gradually alter the phonetic characteristics of phrases,

II. Development of Languages

contributing to the development of unique sound patterns within the isolated group. Over time, this process results in the emergence of a distinct accent, characterized by a particular pronunciation that is unique to the region, area, or social class of the group.

Phoneme Change

The phoneme is the smallest unit of sound that is usually represented by a letter in writing systems. Due to the vocal strain involved in raising one's voice, in a rural mountainous lifestyle phonemes that require blocking the airflow in the vocal tract tend to evolve to allow easier passage of air. This phonetic adaptation facilitates higher sound volume with less respiratory effort.

An example of phoneme shifts can be seen in the transformation of /m/ to /w/ and /v/.

Assimilation

Assimilation occurs when a phoneme changes to become more like a neighboring sound, particularly in rapid speech. For example, in the Kurdish word for 'eight hundred,' 'Heshtsed' /heʃtsed/, the phoneme 'sh' /ʃ/ changes to 's' when followed by 'sed' (Eng. 'hundred'), resulting in /hes-sed/. Another example is the interrogative expression "What do you want?" ('Chet dewet' /tʃet dəʊeət/), where the phoneme /t/ changes to match the following /d/, becoming 'Ched-dewet' /tʃed dəʊeət/.

Elision

Elision, the omission of sounds in rapid speech, has permanently altered many Kurdish words. For example, the Pahlavi word 'Bad' (Eng. 'wind') becomes 'Ba' in modern Kurdish. Similarly, the suffix '-gah' in Pahlavi, denoting premises, changes to '-ga' in modern Kurdish, as seen in words like 'Dadga' (Eng. 'court'), 'Yariga' (Eng. 'stadium'), and 'Froshga' (Eng. 'store'). The word 'Feruxtin' /ferʊːxˈtɪn/ in Pahlavi becomes 'Froshtin' /frɔʃˈtɪn/ in Sorani and 'Firotin' in Kurmanji. In connected speech, final sounds are often omitted, as in 'Dest' (Eng. 'hand'), when followed by a consonant, i.e. in 'Des-xuş' /des'xʊːʃ/ (Eng. 'well done').

Intrusion

Intrusion involves adding an extra sound between consecutive words to ease the utterances, for example, the phrase 'Darek i kesk' (Eng. 'a green tree') adds the sound /j/ between 'Darek' (Eng. 'tree') and 'kesk' (Eng. 'green'), resulting in 'Darek i kesk' (Sor. ' داریکی سەوز ').

Prosodic Traits

Prosody, by a simple definition, is the pronunciation of a group of sounds in a connected speech. It is the rhythm of the language that is found in the variations of loudness, duration, pitch, and pausing. The intonation is a prosodic trait, the discourse-level use of the pitch (Zsiga 2013, p. 68), in a way that language is used to construct connected and meaningful texts.

These phonetic and prosodic features illustrate how Kurdish, like many languages, adapts to its speakers' environments and lifestyles, resulting in significant phonological diversity.

2.1.3 Dialects

A dialect is defined as a form of language that is specific to a particular group of speakers, characterized not only by unique pronunciation but also by distinct grammar and vocabulary. Consequently, isolated groups are influenced by phonological changes and adopt unique accents. Over an extended period, they develop their own syntactic and grammatical rules, leading to the emergence of a distinctive dialect. The longer the isolation persists, the more pronounced the linguistic differences become compared to other dialects. This process represents an early stage in language evolution. The distinction between a dialect and a fully developed language often perplexes linguists, as there is no definitive formula to determine the exact point of divergence. Russian sociolinguist Max

II. Development of Languages

Weinreich succinctly captured this complexity (Laponce, 2005, p. 13) with his statement:

> *"A language is a dialect with an army and navy."*

A similar expression is adopted by the British linguist Randolph Quirk (McArthur, 1998, p. 205):

> *"A language is a dialect with an army and a flag."*

2.1.4 Languages

Dialects evolve in response to group isolation, leading to a gradual decrease in mutual intelligibility over time until cross-dialectal speakers can no longer easily understand each other. At this stage, the dialect is considered a full-fledged language.

Throughout history, human languages have become increasingly complex in order to meet the demands of the ongoing expansion of thoughts and concepts. Modern languages feature advanced grammar, syntax, and deep semantics. Moreover, language has transitioned from purely vocal representation to include orthography, becoming not just a means of personal communication but a phenomenon reflecting social progress and cultural identity. As nations develop, languages evolve, branch into dialects, and die. There is no precise count of how many languages have become extinct throughout history. Some modern languages are vulnerable at present days, such as Belarusian and Chechen; some are considered dead, like Latin and Sanskrit; and some are extinct, such as Aramaic and Gothic. The Scottish writer Gilbert Highet (1906–1978) likened the evolution of language to the lifecycle of a tree:

> *"Language is a living thing. We can feel it changing. Parts of it become old: they drop off and are forgotten. New pieces bud out, spread into leaves, and become big branches, proliferating."*

The Kurdish language is not immune to the risk of partitioning into two or more new languages. Sorani and Kurmanji, with their distinct grammar, syntax, vocabulary, writing systems, literary heritage, and large speaker regions, have the potential to evolve into fully independent languages.

2.1.4.1 Pidgin Languages

Branching is the most common method of language evolution; however, some languages have developed as a means of communication between groups without a common language, such as in colonization settlements and trade regions. The coexistence of non-intelligible varieties without a shared language results in the creation of a new linguistic form characterized by simplified grammatical rules and mixed vocabulary. These languages, known as pidgin languages, serve as a temporary means of communication among groups and are not native to any speakers. Examples of pidgin languages include the extinct American Indian Pidgin English (AIPE), which emerged during the initial contact between Europeans and Native Americans, as well as Sattella in Kenya and Gibanawa in Nigeria.

A pidgin language may eventually become extinct due to changing circumstances or, alternatively, may become a native language for subsequent generations, evolving into a *Creole* language. Examples of Creole languages include Haitian Creole, Andaman Creole Hindi in India, and the Arabic-based Nubi language in Uganda and Kenya.

2.1.4.2 Newborn Languages

Human society is still linguistically fertile; new languages were recently born, such as the West African '*Lingala*' (early 20th century), and the Australian '*Light Warlpiri*' (the 1980s), in addition to the linguistically designed *Esperanto* (1887). (*)

---

* 5 of the World's Newest Languages." Grammar.com. STANDS4 LLC, 2024. Web. 10 Feb. 2024.
<https://www.grammar.com/5_of_the_world's_newest_languages>

II. Development of Languages

Languages are dynamic and constantly evolving, with new languages emerging as sociocultural, economic, and technological conditions change. While it is challenging to predict specific future languages, there are several contexts in which new languages could potentially emerge, like sociolinguistic developments, globalization, and excessive urbanization.

2.2 Linguistic Instability

Languages are in a state of continual self-modification, with diachronic changes in grammar and shifts in sounds and semantics being transmitted from generation to generation. A review of literary works produced over past centuries reveals that languages have undergone constant updates, reflecting variations in historical circumstances such as changes in economic, social, and cultural status. Furthermore, waves of immigration, wars, and the spread of religious doctrines significantly influence linguistic habits. As social progress is a persistent and unending process, the complexity of thoughts and ideas communicated within a society increases over time, prompting languages to enhance their grammatical, syntactical, phonological, and morphological tools accordingly.

For instance, the English language has evolved so significantly over the last five centuries that modern native speakers often struggle to comprehend Shakespeare's plays without proper interpretation. Additionally, Old English manuscripts from a few centuries earlier are perceived as foreign texts that require translation for contemporary understanding. The epic poem Beowulf, composed around the eighth century, exemplifies diachronic variation.

Original verses:

"*Hwæt. We Gardena in geardagum,*
þeodcyninga, þrym gefrunon,
hu ða æþelingas ellen fremedon.
Oft Scyld Scefing sceaþena þreatum,"

Modern English translation:

> "*LO, praise of the prowess of people-kings*
> *of spear-armed Danes, in days long sped,*
> *we have heard, and what honor the athelings won!*
> *Oft Scyld the Scefing from squadroned foes,"* (*)

Similarly, the Kurdish language has undergone significant changes throughout its history. Compared to three centuries ago, there are noticeable phonetic biases. According to the 18th-century missionary M. Garzoni's Kurdish-Italian dictionary, words like 'Du' (two), 'Sê' (three), and 'Çar' (four) were listed as 'Duh', 'Seh', and 'Ciahr' /tʃahr/, respectively. The latter was mentioned by MacKenzie as 'čahăr' /tʃahar/ in the sixth-century Pahlavi. Other words have also shown clear biases, such as 'Kevok' (pigeon), listed by Garzoni as 'Kefter', while in Pahlavi, it was noted as 'kabōd' and 'kabōtar' (MacKenzie, 1971, p. 21, 127). Additionally, the phrase 'Min got' (Eng. *I said*) was recorded as 'Men ghot' (Garzoni M., 1787, p. 17, 37, 213).

This continuous evolution reflects how languages adapt to the changing needs and influences of their speakers over time.

2.2.1 Balance of Complexity

On one side, more advanced grammar and a more detailed vocabulary enable a language to convey complex and nuanced thoughts with greater accuracy. On the other side, expanding the lexicon and grammatical rules introduces further linguistic complexity, requiring additional attention to rules, restrictions, and meticulous conceptualization. This linguistic advancement generates intricacies such as sophisticated infrequent patterns, increased learning difficulty, and the potential emergence of sociolects. In

---

* Translated by Francis B. Gummere
<poetryfoundation.org/poems/50114/beowulf-modern-english-translation>

II. Development of Languages

simple terms, eloquent expression becomes linguistically demanding. Consequently, in slow-progressing environments, languages tend to economize effort by discarding unnecessary patterns.

As social demands increase and communication needs become more sophisticated, a society naturally expands its language rules. The size and eloquence of a language are influenced by the extent of social advancement and common thoughts. Language functions like a virtual vehicle that transfers notions and ideas between interlocutors or from writer to reader.

The expansion of sociocultural phenomena necessitates the growth of language, leading to the accumulation of more vocabulary and the adoption of detailed grammatical rules. Without this expansion, language would not sustain the burden of extra rules and might even shrink in more primitive expressions. To illustrate, when conveying an idea from point A to point B, a lighter, faster, and cheaper vehicle (a simpler lexicon and grammar) is optimal for reducing costs and complexity. However, for more complex ideas (heavier), a larger, more costly vehicle (a larger lexicon and more advanced grammar) is required. By costly grammar, we refer to the use of more complicated rules that are harder to learn while demanding greater attention to detail. Thus, the advancement of science and knowledge necessitates more sophisticated linguistic capabilities.

This concept illustrates the necessity for language tools to be modified or updated based on the complexity of the exchanged thoughts. Constant changes in lifestyle, the progress of science and religion, the accumulation of experiences, and the introduction of new industrial products impose significant demands on communication, necessitating linguistic modifications.

To exemplify linguistic austerity, some primitive tribes in Western Africa and South America have not developed more than twelve phonemes (the smallest sound unit). Professor Daniel Everett (2012) noted that the language of the indigenous Brazilian (Amazon Basin) tribe "Pirahã" contains only eleven phonemes, three of which are vowels, while the remaining eight consonants are used by males and only seven by females. Nevertheless, their language is sufficient for their needs and is not at risk of extinction, as the tribe is not bilingual. Conversely, the Scientific Revolution in the 16th and 17th centuries, and its impact on social development, necessitated enriching languages, especially in Western Europe, leading to qualitative shifts and even radical changes, such as those observed in Russian, Turkish, Chinese, and Kurdish.

2.2.2 Natural Selection

Language equilibrium inherently involves a Darwinian selection process that determines the survival or extinction of linguistic patterns based on their utility. Jacob Marschak (1965) referred to this phenomenon as the "economy of language," where languages operate as a continuous optimization process. The German sociolinguist Florian Coulmas (2020, p. 76) cited Marschak's view on the dynamic development of languages as a natural selection of linguistic traits:

> *"Marschak goes on to argue that certain traits of languages have more chances of surviving in the long term because they represent a solution to such a trade-off, while others tend to disappear over time."*

This observation implies that numerous obsolete Kurdish words have disappeared over the past centuries. Recovering a list of these archaic words is crucial for tracing the morphological roots of contemporary vocabulary. However, this task is challenging due to the scarcity of comprehensive and scientifically rigorous research on diachronic linguistic analysis.

II. Development of Languages

2.2.3 Modern Requirements

During the Dark Ages, language development was predominantly influenced by religious institutions, which emphasized rhetoric and ambiguity to align with metaphysical mythologies. In contrast, the advancement of science required greater precision in the communication of ideas and data. The ancient Greeks transformed human language from imprecise forms to sophisticated structures, and the Renaissance further accelerated scientific progress, necessitating even more precise language for conveying information.

Following the invention of the printing press, the proliferation of reading habits marked a significant evolution in the use of language, adding a new medium in addition to oral communication. By the end of the 15th century, printing presses had produced an estimated five million books across Europe for a population of approximately 61 million people (Barzun et al., 2024), with this number increasing to 200 million books by the year 1600. (*) This quantum leap had a profound impact on human languages, promoting formal standards over colloquial forms and orthography over phonetics.

Modern technological advancements have introduced numerous new items like tools, crops, and commodities that require to be dubbed and named, further expanding lexicons. Sociocultural developments have also left their mark on lifestyles, requiring languages to continuously adapt. By the start of the 20th century, many languages had undergone changes to avoid decline. Notable examples include German standardization in 1901, Russian reform in 1917, the compilation of the English Oxford Dictionary in 1928, Chinese simplification in 1949, and various linguistic modifications in the Soviet Union, Asia, and Africa.

Since the turn of the 21st century, languages have faced a new wave of challenges to accommodate scientific advancement and the naming of a new generation of products, maintaining, at the same time, the

---

* According to Statista, it is a global data and business intelligence platform with an extensive collection of statistics, reports, and insights.
<http:///www.statista.com/statistics/1396121/europe-book-production-half-century-region-historical>

level of fluency and ease of use. Among the solutions through which this qualitative leap was accommodated incorporating abbreviated vocabulary resulting from the rise of texting on social media, achieving greater precision in expressions, and adapting to increased population migration and the unprecedented fusion of languages.

This dynamic evolution reflects the ongoing need for the Kurdish languages to adapt and evolve in response to changing societal and technological contexts.

2.2.4 Death of Languages

As language is a dynamic entity, emerging under specific historical circumstances and fading under others, some languages, such as Latin and Slavic, gradually faded out by branching into new languages, while others, like Elamite, Sumerian, Akkadian, and Aramaic, vanished abruptly due to historical events. The regions of Mesopotamia and the Zagros Mountains are notable for their many extinct languages. Invasions, large-scale migrations, cultural assimilation, and the decline of religious doctrines have all contributed to the disappearance of these languages.

The term "dead language" refers to a language that is still in use but no longer native to any community, such as Latin, which is used symbolically in the Vatican. Conversely, "extinct language" denotes a language that has no native speakers and no modern descendant languages, such as Old Egyptian. The death of a language is often a precursor to its extinction. However, some liturgical languages can be revived after centuries, as demonstrated by Hebrew. The language was revitalized in the late 19th century, largely due to the efforts of Russian Jewish linguist Eliezer Ben-Yehuda (1858–1922).

In the 20th century alone, 110 languages became extinct, and in the first decade of the 21st century, 12 languages were declared dead. (*) According to UNESCO, there are almost 2500 languages around the

---

* Statistics from Zing Languages. <https://www.zinglanguages.com/how-many-languages-in-the-world/#12-extinct-languages>

II. Development of Languages

world in danger of extinction (*) with 27 of these languages spoken in the Northern Areas of Pakistan. (†)

Kurdish, which originated from Pahlavi, has developed and branched into various dialects. Without appropriate measures to unify these formal dialects, the language risks disintegration into several new languages, similar to the historical branching of Sanskrit, Pahlavi, and Latin. Despite appearing as a relatively young language, Kurdish is a candidate for further fragmentation.

2.3 Linguistic Interference

In bilingual communities, language interference leads to the mutual adaptation of linguistic norms across phonological, semantic, syntactic, and lexical levels, driven by the speakers' familiarity with each other's language. The extent of this interference is influenced by several factors, including the degree of fluency in the second language (L2) and the level of linguistic genealogical kinship, where languages share similar grammatical and morphological structures. This phenomenon, as described by Uriel Weinreich (1953), is characterized as the deviation from the norms of one language due to the influence of another, resulting from prolonged contact.

> *"The term interference implies the rearrangement of patterns that result from the introduction of foreign elements into the more highly structured domains of language, such as the bulk of the phonemic system, a large part of the morphology and syntax, and some areas of the vocabulary (kinship, color, weather, etc."*

In other cases, a deliberate unilateral influence imposes certain linguistic norms over others planned by assimilation policies and is

---

* Atlas of the World's Languages in Danger. UNESCO, 2011
† Dawn (Pakistani newspaper). 22 February 2011

imposed by outsiders. Exposure to different occupant authorities that follow a planned assimilation process results in the adoption of different linguistic norms in different speaking regions. This explains the influence of Turkish in NE. and Arabic in Roj., despite the lack of a genealogical or semantic affinity with Kurdish. In the East., however, the Kurdish dialects were heavily influenced by Persian, the Iranic sister, for genealogical relations and common morphological structures more than the assimilation policies. The obvious signs of influence are word borrowing, the literal translation of modern terms (see Section 2.3.2), and code-switching. On the other hand, the lack of interaction among language varieties, i.e., remote linguistic development, exacerbates mutual unintelligibility. This phenomenon explains the remarkable diachronic divergence of Kurdish dialects.

2.3.1 Word Borrowing

Scientific inventions, modern discoveries, and social transformations often necessitate lexical expansion in languages. When a new concept or entity emerges without an existing term, languages may either create new words or borrow from each other. Word borrowing is a prevalent phenomenon indicative of linguistic interference. For instance, it is estimated that 29% of modern English vocabulary originates from French, another 29% from Latin, while only 26% comes from Germanic origins, including Old English.

In Kurdistan, the introduction of the refrigerator led to the borrowing of terms from dominant neighboring languages due to the absence of an indigenous word. Thus, 'Yakhchal' from Persian, 'Thalaja' from Iraqi Arabic, 'Barrad' from Syrian Arabic, and 'Buzdolabı' from Turkish were adopted in various regions. Similarly, foreign terms like 'car', 'ticket', 'airplane', and 'airport' are commonly found differently in different Kurdish-speaking regions.

Globally, technological advancements continuously introduce new terms into living languages. The advent of 'radio', 'telephone', and 'television' was followed by terms like 'WI-FI', 'mobile', 'chat', and 'internet', which have quickly spread worldwide. Languages vary in their acceptance of foreign words; some craft native equivalents, while others adopt them with phonetic adjustments.

II. Development of Languages

Religious and cultural influences also contribute to lexical interference. For instance, Arabic vocabulary has penetrated languages spoken by Muslim majorities, with terms like 'Inshallah' (God willing), 'Tawbah' (Repentance), and 'Thawab' (Recompense). Turkish influence during the Ottoman Empire introduced terms still used in southern Kurdistan, such as 'boyunbağı' (tie), 'bardak' (cup), and 'kız' (girl).

Nativization Policy

The influence of neighboring languages is not limited to grammar and lexicon, the ideology of the Kurdish language is also affected and varies regionally

While Persian policy tolerates foreign words, restrictive nativization policies in Arabic and Turkish encourage the creation of native terms rather than borrowing. For example, worldwide common words such as 'Committee', 'Automobile', and 'Radio' are borrowed as-is in some languages, while others create native synonyms. These words were Turkified in Turkey to become 'Kurul', 'Araba', and 'Telsiz', and Arabized to 'اللجنة' /lidʒn-nəh/, 'سيارة' /sə'jaːr-rəh/, and 'مذياع' /mɪðˈjaːʕ/. However, since Persian policy is more open to foreign words, it borrows terms like 'کمیته' /kʌmjːt-təh/, 'ماشین' /mɒʃjn/, and 'رادیو' /radˈjʊ/.

Thus, comparing the Sorani in both regions East and South, we notice the passive mentality with the former. Words are literarily borrowed, such as 'University' as 'دانشگاه' /danɪʃ-gaːh/ and 'Airport' as 'فرودگاه' /fʊrʊdˈgaːh/, unlike the natively derived equivalents in the South as 'زانکۆ' /zãːnkɒ/ and 'فڕۆکەخانە' /ˈfrɒkəxaːnəh/.

The variant level of Kurdification as a nativizing policy adds another source of divergence on the dialectal level; practical unification of Kurdish standards required unity of linguistic ideology too.

Analogical Changes

In addition to pronunciation changes and borrowing words, new words may evolve as a result of analogical changes such as verbing. For instance, the popular expression 'God willing' (Sor. خوا بکا /xwa:

bka:/) is converted into a verb /xwa:bka:/ to mean *hope*. A person in Arbil may add the first person pronoun suffix 'm' (خوابکەم) to convert it to a verb, as in 'I am hoping'.

2.3.2 Literal Wording

Literal translation relies on straightforward synonymy, rendering a term word-for-word based on its roots and bypassing the conceptual structure. Literal wording is coining a native phrase that literally mimics the meaning rather than borrowing the exact words.

Take the word 'Institute', for instance, it is Kurdified in the South by the literal translation of the Arabic 'معهد' /məʕ‚həd/. This word is derived from the polysemous stem 'عهد' /ʕəhɪd/, (Eng. 'Convent', 'Promise', and 'Era') by the standard locative meter 'مفعل' /məfʕəl/ to mean the place of convent or promise. The cognate was coined from 'پەیمان' /peɪˈmaːn/ (Eng. promise) followed by the locative suffix 'گا' /gaː/ (denotes the place of) to simulate the literal meaning (place of promise).

Since Kurdish linguistic policy differs regionally, this nomenclature may be unanticipated in the North, retaining 'enstîtû', and in the East borrowing the exact Persian 'موسسه' /muːʔəˈssəsə/ (Eng. foundation) or 'مرکز اموزش' /ˈmərkəz ɪ ˈaːmuːzɪʃ/ (Eng. 'learning center').

Likewise, the word 'Stadium' is Kurdified as 'یاریگا' /jˈaːrjːgaː/ following the same Arabic locative meter 'ملعب' /melːˈʕeb/ of the stem 'لعب' /ləʕɪb/ Eng 'Play', coined as stem 'یاری' /jaɾi/ followed by the locative suffix 'گا' /ˈgaː/. The word 'Province' 'پارێزگا' /pəɾəzgaːh/, a Kurdish synonym of the Arabic 'Muahfaza' with the literal meaning of 'Retention' (Kurm. 'Herêm' and Eastern Sor. 'استان' /ʊsˈtaːn/). Thus, 'Governer' 'پارێزگار' /pəɾəzˈgaːr/ (Kurm. 'Walî' and Eastern Sor. 'استاندار' /ʊsˈtaːndar/), similates 'Muhafiz' Eng. Retentive.

As Kurdish, across international borders, is influenced by different policies, following multiple development routes, further divergence is feasible, and as such, mutual intelligibility is getting harder over time. This diversity of resources, in the long run, overburdens social communication within the Kurdish-speaking populations, future

II. Development of Languages

hardening attempts at unification and modernization. Thus, it is essential for linguistic unity to unify and standardize the policy of borrowing words and literal wording.

Since the large scale of word borrowing denotes submitting to external influences, reducing the stratum of the language; conservative cultures reluctantly accept foreign words and tend to nativize the terms. Elites in certain political systems raise the banner of linguistic purism for various reasons, such as:

- Rise of national sentiments after independence (e.g. *Norwegian*).
- The need for a single official language (e.g. *Filipino*)
- Major social shifts such as the collapse of the Ottoman empire (e.g. *Turkish*).
- Religious motivations for archaizing purism (*e.g. Arabic*).
- Save an endangered language (*e.g. Kurdish*).

2.4 Logical Structure

The implications of empiricism theory, (*) dating back to Francis Bacon in the early 17th century, effectively separated science from religious affairs. The resultant surge in scientific production gradually supplanted interpretive ambiguity with the clarity characteristic of scientific descriptive language. Prior to this, linguistic expressions were deliberately flexible to accommodate the varied interpretations inherent in religious texts. In contrast, scientific

---

* The Empiricism Theory, founded by F. Bacon (1561-1626), is a philosophical approach that emphasizes the role of observations and sensory experience in the formation of knowledge, rejecting all metaphysical interpretations and notions, including religious doctrines.

writing necessitates verbal precision that precludes multiple interpretations, thus imposing new demands on language. This transition from ambiguity to explicit meaning required the development of more detailed grammatical structures and the clarification of verbal connotations, aiming to cover concepts with greater precision. Abrahamic religions deny the evolution of languages, viewing them as a collection of predefined concepts originating externally. For instance, according to the Old Testament, (*) God created incomprehensible languages to thwart the construction of the Tower of Babel, preventing humanity from reaching Paradise. The Islamic perception also holds that God taught Adam the language. (†) However, during the Age of Enlightenment, the concept of 'language' was secularized. Sacredness and liturgical reference were rejected by prominent philosophers; for Thomas Hobbes, senses are no longer Platonian but rather conceptualized based on human perception (Creet P. A. R., 1954, p. 11); and for John Locke, words are merely to convey information about the contents of the speaker's thought.

By the early 20th century, philosophers identified linguistic deficiencies as a primary reason for the ambiguous interpretation of thought and a significant cause of failure in philosophical studies. German mathematician Gottlob Frege (1919, p. 362) asserted that thought depends on language, which in turn can distort thought. He explained his concern with language in his quest for a mathematical and logical foundation:

> *"The logical imperfections of language stood in the way of such investigations. I tried to overcome these obstacles with my begriffsschrift [concept-script]. In this way, I was led from mathematics to logic."*

One of the most controversial approaches emerged from Austrian philosopher Ludwig Wittgenstein, who attributed philosophical problems to misunderstandings of linguistic logic:

> *"I believe, that the reason why these problems are posed is that the logic of our language is misunderstood."* (Wittgenstein, 1922)

---

* Book of Genesis 11:1-9
† Quran 2:31

II. Development of Languages

Both Frege and Wittgenstein, along with English philosopher Bertrand Russell, articulated the philosophy of logical atomism, wherein language is viewed as an aggregate of discrete irreducible units akin to atoms. Thus, sentences must be logically analyzed at the atomic level to achieve logical clarity. This principle implies that if a sentence contains any false element, it is considered false, regardless of syntactical correctness. Russell (1905) illustrated this with the sentence:

"The present king of France is bold."

At the time this sentence was written, there was no king in the Republic of France. Therefore, although it is syntactically valid, it is considered false. Similarly, the following sentence is also considered false:

*"The present king of France is **not** bold."*

This logical analysis imposes an additional complexity on language. However, transforming the sentence into a logical proposition is a step toward developing a universal rule for an ideal language, in which factual accuracy is integrated into grammatical structure.

Russell's argument might appear impractical as it surpasses the current functional capacity of language. Nonetheless, incorporating the meaning of a sentence into its grammar is feasible in some languages, such as English and Spanish, through the use of verb moods. These moods indicate the speaker's attitude and help convey emotional states to the audience. The subjunctive mood, for instance, explores wishes, desires, and hypothetical actions that may not reflect reality within the specified grammatical framework.

III. Evolution of Kurdish

"If you talk to a man in a language he understands, that goes to his head. If you talk to him in his own language, that goes to his heart."

Nelson Mandela

The Kurdish-speaking region, located at the heart of the Middle East, is significant both politically and culturally, warranting greater scholarly attention than it currently receives. However, The linguistic research on Kurdish is sparse and lacks robust support, with genealogical analyses being rare and often intertwined with ethnographic opinions. The prevailing theory posits that Kurdish belongs to the Indo-Iranian branch of the Indo-European language family (McCarus, 1958), with substantial evidence suggesting it descends from Pahlavi. Another perspective, however, suggests a remote connection to the Chaldean group (Fossum, 1919, p. 6)

3.1 Roots

Hypothetically, the spread of Indo-European languages originated from Anatolia and northern Kurdistan, coinciding with the expansion of farming approximately nine thousand years ago (Bouckaert et al., 2013). The Anatolian hypothesis, first proposed by British archaeologist Colin Renfrew in 1987, posits that speakers of Proto-

Indo-European (PIE) resided in Anatolia during the Neolithic era. This hypothesis links the dispersion of historical Indo-European languages to the Neolithic Revolution of the 7th and 6th millennia BC. However, an alternative hypothesis, which has garnered broader academic support, disputes the Anatolian origin.

According to the Kurgan hypothesis proposed by Professor Marija Gimbutas (1974, p. 34), the homeland of PIE speakers extended over the Pontic-Caspian steppe. The PIE language is believed to have been spoken as a single language during the Late Neolithic to Early Bronze Age (4500–2500 BCE). Yet, migration waves dispersed these tribes, creating daughter languages. While some groups moved west and north (Latin, Germanic, Slavic), those moving eastward formed the Indo-Iranian languages.

"*The breakdown of the Indo-Iranian branch into Indian and Iranian occurred somewhere between 2000 and 1600 BCE when future Indians left their tribesmen and crossed the Hindu Kush on their way to India...*" (Lubotsky, 2020, p. 6).

Proto-Iranic speakers headed towards the Iranian plateau, where Pahlavi started to develop as an administrative language for the Iranian empires and the liturgical language of Zoroastrianism until the Muslim Arab tribes invaded the plateau in the seventh century. Subsequently, the language started to decline and modern Persian, Pashto, Baluchi, and Kurdish, along with other smaller varieties emerged and became dominant in their respective regions. The decline of Zoroastrianism stripped the Pahlavi of its sacred state; this, along with losing the Sasanian power, pushed the western Iranic tribes to further isolate themselves in the rugged landscape of the Zagros mountains for the course of a millennium. Besides, the synchronous advance of urban life switched to using a foreign language (Arabic) as liturgical, not only for religious affairs but also in literature and documentation. This neglect and prolonged isolation led to significant linguistic divergence, culminating in the contemporary Kurdish language with its diverse dialects.

The decline of Pahlavi and the failure to establish a replacement hindered the natural evolution of a cohesive national identity. Historically, Kurdish scholars showed little interest in linguistic fields, often favoring Arabic for their documentary, religious, and

III. Evolution of Kurdish

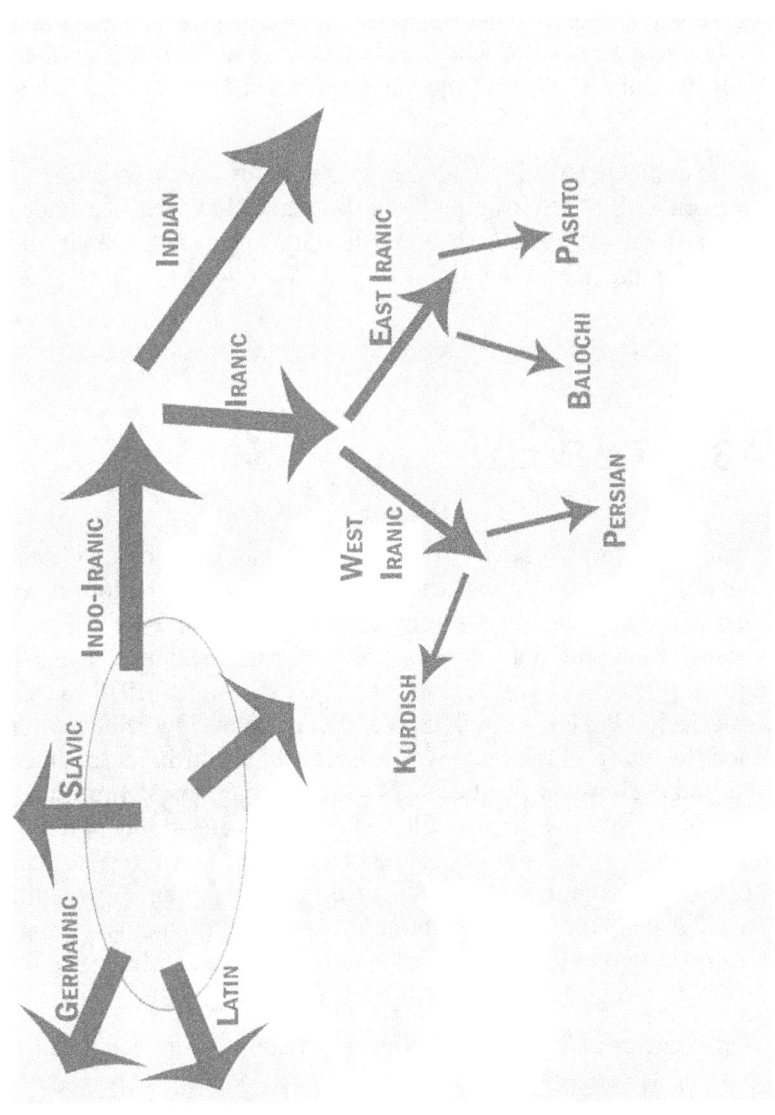

Evolution of Kurdish according to Kurgan hypothesis.

philosophical works. For instance, even in the 18th century poet Ali Taramokhi authored a Kurdish book on grammar that focused more on Arabic grammar for Kurdish students than on Kurdish grammar itself, teaching in his mosque and Quranic Madrasah in his village Teremox.

This preference for foreign languages not only accelerated Kurdish divergence from other Iranic-based languages but further distanced Kurdish dialects from each other, leading to greater diversity and reducing mutual intelligibility.

3.2 The Pahlavi

Pahlavi, alongside ancient Greek and Syriac, was one of the few advanced languages in the extensive Middle Eastern region. It was used as a liturgical language by Zoroastrianism and for scientific studies at late antiquity universities such as Ctesiphon (Baghdad), Edessa (Urfa), and Gundeshapur (Ahvaz) (Spengler, 1918, p. 63). Historically, Pahlavi served as a conduit of knowledge, transmitting scientific and philosophical works from China and India to Greece and Rome. However, its decline began following the Islamization of the Iranian plateau in the 7th century AD, coinciding with the restriction of its use and the destruction of universities, temples, and libraries. A century later, much of the pre-Islamic scientific knowledge in fields such as astronomy, chemistry, anatomy, biology, botany, cosmology, mathematics, engineering, and architecture was hidden or lost.

On the verge of losing such a scientific treasure, prominent Pahlavi-speaking scientists and philosophers such as Avicenna, Abu Bakr al-Razi, Al-Khwarizmi, and Abu Nasr al-Farabi managed to reproduce some of this knowledge. However, under the Abbasid Caliphate, these reproductions were exclusively written in Arabic, which had become the dominant liturgical language. Consequently, Pahlavi lost its prestige and position as the language of science and scholarship. This decline led to its fragmentation, similar to Latin during the Enlightenment era, resulting in the emergence of modern Kurdish,

III. Evolution of Kurdish

Persian, Pashto, and Baluchi. These languages developed in isolation, leading to increased linguistic diversity across the Iranian plateau. Although Kurdish retained much of its inherited lexicon with minimal borrowing from foreign languages, it lost its orthography and shifted to Arabic for written contributions and academic usage. This lack of a writing system led to linguistic deviations, such as phonetic biases, shifts in phonemes, and phonological changes in morphemes. The abandonment of Pahlavi in writing and the decline of its academic variety caused the language to lose many of its aspects, becoming a burden for its speakers. For the less urbanized tribes in the rugged Zagros region, isolation contributed to significant dialectal differences, reducing mutual intelligibility over time. Additionally, constant warfare, whether defensive or tribal, characterized the lifestyle of the population and hindered the establishment of scientific institutions, preventing Kurdish from emerging as a unified academic language.

3.3 Colloquial Kurdish

A vernacular develops as an oral means of communication without strict grammatical rules or precise vocabulary definitions. This flexibility renders it susceptible to environmental influences and changes in linguistic patterns. Therefore, adopting linguistic standards as a formal variety helps regulate colloquial changes by preserving grammatical rules, pronunciation, and word and phrase definitions. This regulation protects the language from further sound shifts, similar to the following:

/d/: The alveolar stop consonant shifts to the approximant 'y' /j/, as in 'Leadan' /lɪəˈdɑːn/ (Sorani: 'لێدان' , meaning 'to beat'), which becomes 'Leayan' /lɪəˈjɑːn/ (Sorani: 'لێیان').

/b/: The Pahlavi term 'Sheb' /ʃəb/ (Eng. 'night') transforms to 'Shew' /ʃeʊ/ in Sorani and 'Shev' /ʃəv/ in Kurmanji.

/m/: A well-known example is the Indo-European morpheme 'Nam' (Eng. 'name') that changes to 'Naw' /naʊ/ in Sorani and 'Nav' /nav/

in Kurmanji. This transformation also occurs in borrowed terms, such as the Arabic 'Temam' becoming 'Tewaw', and 'Salam' changing to 'Slaw' and 'Slav'.

/h/: The voiceless glottal fricative consonant 'h' is replaced with the vowel 'a' in words like 'Tehran', pronounced 'Taran'. The term 'Bahane' /bəhɑːne/ (Eng. 'occasion') is altered to 'Bone' /ˈbɔnə/ (Sorani: بۆنە).

/z/: The sound 'z' transforms to 'zh' /ʒ/ (as in the sound of Eng. 'pleasure'). For example, 'Ruz' (Eng. 'day') in 'Newruz' changes to 'rozh' /rɔʒ/ (Sorani: 'ڕۆژ'). Similarly, 'Namaz' (Eng. 'prayer') changes to 'Newej' /nʊːˈɪəʒ/ (Sor. 'نوێژ').

The shift of the phoneme /m/ to /v/ and /w/ is illustrated by comparing the Kurdish word for 'name' (Kurm. "Nav," Sor. "Naw") with its counterparts in Indo-European languages, showing a stem composed of the consonants 'N' and 'M,' with a vowel in the middle.

Language	Form	Sound
Persian	نام	/naːm/
Hindi/Urdu	नाम / نام	/naːm/
Bangali	নাম	/naːm/
Pashto	نوم	/nuːm/
Belochi	نام	/naːm/
German	Name	/naːme/
French	Nom	/nɔm/
Italian	Nome	/nɔme/
Dutch	Naam	/naːm/

This phonemic shift is also evident in borrowed words. For instance, the Arabic-origin word 'Salam' (used as an equivalent to 'Hello') is borrowed with minimal alteration by many Middle Eastern languages such as Turkish, Persian, and Urdu. However, in Kurdish, it transforms into Kurm. 'Slav' and Sor. 'Slaw'. Other phonemes affected by the absence of formal linguistic standards include /d/, /b/, /z/, and /h/.

III. Evolution of Kurdish

The table below illustrates the comparison of these phonemes in Pahlavi and their derivatives in the two current formal Kurdish dialects:

	Phalavi [*]	Kurmanji	Sorani	سۆرانی	English
B	Ab	Av	Aw	ئاو	Water
	Şab	Şev	Şew	شەو	Night
	Sêb	Sêv	Sêw	سێو	Apple
	Lab	Lêv	Lêw	لێو	Lip
D	bûdan	bûyin	bûn	بوون	Become
	Zûd	Zû	Zû	زو	Quick
	Zard	Zer	Zard	زەرد	Yellow
	Sard	Sar	Sard	سارد	Cold
M	Nam	Nav	Naw	ناو	Name
	Çaşm	Çav	Çaw	چاو	Eye
	Mehman	Mêvan	Mêwan	میوان	Guest
	Ham (hemwelati)	Hev (hevwelatî)	Haw (hawelati)	هاوڵاتی	Co- (prefix)
H	Şah (Padşa)	Şa	Paşa	پاشا	King
	Çahar	Çar	Çwar	چوار	Four
	Dadgah	Dadgeh	Dadga	دادگا	Court
	Şahr	(Bajar) Şar	Şar	شار	City
Z	Namaz	Nivêj	Nwêj	نوێژ	Prayer
	Draz	Dirêj	Drêj	درێژ	Long
	Roz	Roj	Roj	ڕۆژ	Day
SH	Rêş	Rî	Rîş	ریش	Beard
	Roşn	Ronî	Ronak	ڕووناک	Bright

[*](MacKenzie, 1971)

The most phonological changes occurred on phonemes that required blocking the airflow—that is, constraining the respiratory passage through the oral cavity. When non-initial voiced plosive phonemes, especially the bilabial /b/, the alveolar /d/, and the nasal /m/ hold the breath (exhaling), it creates pressure on the lung, which hinders loud utterances. The respiratory anticipation is hypothesized to ensure that speakers have enough air to produce the upcoming utterance without going below the resting expiratory level (REL).(Włodarczak & Heldner, 2017) These phonetic shifts occur to suit life in a presumably ragged mountainous terrain and are an example of the environmental impact behind the evolution of Kurdish.

3.3.2 Dialects

The linguistic divergence within Kurdish presents a significant obstacle to achieving the unity of the language, potentially surpassing acceptable levels of cohesion. In contrast to languages such as Spanish and Portuguese, Kurdish dialects exhibit lesser mutual intelligibility. Additionally, these dialects, represented primarily by Sorani and Kurmanji, employ distinct alphabetical, morphological, and syntactical structures, along with varying grammatical conventions. Each dialect has cultivated its own literary tradition, yet none have attained independent language status. The recognition of a dialect as a distinct language necessitates a notable cultural divergence, a criterion yet to be met by Sorani and Kurmanji despite differences in orthography.

The preservation of Kurdish linguistic integrity is hindered by ongoing social circumstances across Kurdish-speaking regions, which have not sufficiently diverged to catalyze sociocultural fragmentation among populations. However, while Kurdish unity is lauded by enthusiasts, it does not preclude the natural evolution of dialects into distinct languages, particularly if remedial efforts are neglected.

Divided by international borders, the geopolitical division of the Kurdish homeland contributes to divergent cultural developments, with linguistic ramifications leading to disparate regional progressions over time. Furthermore, the absence of a standardized writing system, including a unified dictionary, reinforces distinct linguistic identities, facilitating the evolution of dialects into regional ethnolects across diverse speaker landscapes.

3.3.3 Ethnolects

An ethnolect refers to the linguistic variety spoken by members of a distinctive ethnic group within a broader language community. Examples include African-American Vernacular English (AAVE) and the historical Arabic of Iraqi Jews. The term was first used to describe the dialects of ethnic immigrant groups from non-English-speaking regions in America. Australian linguist Michael Clyne defines an ethnolect as a variety that emerges from a declining minority language within the majority language context. He specifically cites AAVE and Greek-Australian as examples, highlighting that as the minority language use declines, its symbolic significance as an identity marker shifts to a variety of the majority language employed by the minority group:

> *"As the use of a minority language declines, in the second generation and beyond, its symbolic significance as an identity marker is transferred to a variety of the majority language, the variety which is employed by the minority group"* (*)

Ethnic identity refers to the collective sense of belonging to a group or subgroup with a common cultural background, emphasizing self-identification and personal choice since it is defined as one's own evaluation and sense of self. (†) The increasing diversity and emergence of isolated identities within the Kurdish-speaking population encourage these groups to transform their dialects into ethnolects, fostering pride and a sense of distinction. While linguistic variations are common in many languages and often seen as linguistic richness, Kurdish lacks a unique formal variety recognized as a collective standard by Kurds or linguists. For instance, Google Translate, despite utilizing the latest technical knowledge of *Neural Machine Translation*, could not merge the two main dialects in a

---

* Clyne, M. G. (2000). Lingua franca and ethnolects in Europe and beyond. Sociolinguistica. Vol 1. page 86.

† George A. Akerlof, Rachel E. Kranton. Economics and identity. The Quarterly Journal of Economics. Volume 115. Issue 3. August 2000. Pages 715, https://doi.org/10.1162/003355300554881

single formal form, offering, unlike other languages, two entries for Kurdish instead of one.

An ethnolect serves as a crucial marker of an ethnic group's identity, significantly contributing to the distinctiveness of its characteristics. Given that Kurdish dialects are geographically isolated, internationally separated, and influenced by diverse cultural backgrounds; the speakers of a variety of lifestyle, religion, linguistics, and sociocultural advancement accentuate the sense of a distinct ethnic identity.

The division of the Kurdish-speaking population by international borders results in each segment evolving under the influence of the dominant culture of its respective country. The northern region experiences significant Turkification, while the eastern part is influenced by radical Islamic Persian culture, and the southern part undergoes Arabization. These sociocultural influences, along with differing levels of public freedoms, women's rights, and education among Turkey, Iran, and Arab regions, contribute to the divergence of Kurdish cultures.

Additionally, the development of linguistic norms is influenced by varying economic conditions, purchasing power parity, and the rural-urban population ratio. Kurdish society's religious and sectarian diversity also plays a role in shaping ethnic identities. The Zaza dialect is associated with Alavism, while Kurmanji and Sorani speakers predominantly follow the Sunni-Shafie doctrine, and Pahlawani speakers in the east are mainly Shiite Muslims. Other religious groups, such as Ezedis, Shabaks, and Yarsanis, as well as diasporic minorities like Christians, Jews, and Zoroastrians, each contribute to linguistic diversity.

A dialect with an established writing system that gains a superstratum status and geographical independence may evolve into an ethnolect as part of natural linguistic evolution. For instance, Kurmanji, if conceptualized as an ethnic marker, has the potential to be recognized as an independent language. Sorani and Zaza also possess the necessary attributes for such recognition, while Pahlawani, lacking an orthographic system, might merge with Persian, similar to Luri, under cultural pressure and due to their close genealogical kinship.

III. Evolution of Kurdish

3.4 Future of Kurdish

The farming and semi-nomadic lifestyle of the eighteenth century may have enriched Kurdish with fabulous folk tales, engrossing poems about the summer breeze passing through the mountainous hills and cool orchards, and may have coined wisdom proverbs and myths. However, within that linguistic framework, society would not produce a sufficient level of communication skills to keep pace with the rapid progression of the modern civic lifestyle in today's Kermanshah, Diyarbakir, or Erbil. It does not meet the demands of scientific studies, economics, law, and administrative needs of the twenty-first century. A language requires continual updates to align with changes in lifestyle since the language, viewed as a living organism, must evolve to incorporate new developments, as posited by Greek Professor S. A. Paipetis:

> *"By considering language as an entity functioning according to the rules of natural selection, we prove that language is actually a living organism, behaving in the same genetic way as every other living creature."* (*)

For Kurdish to endure in the forthcoming centuries, it must meet contemporary needs for exchanging complex ideas and precise information. To achieve this, a unified, formal, advanced form of the standardized dialect is essential. Without such standardization, the language risks obsolescence in the light of linguistic competition in the Middle East. The modification of both Kurmanji and Sorani in the post-WW1 era has saved the language and kept both dialects fit throughout the last century, while with the absence of a unified standard dialect as a recognized formal variety, none of the two has gained the required prestige or popularity among other dialects or even been considered as a source for loan words. Currently, Kurdish

---

* Paipetis S.A (2019). Language as a Living Entity. Journal of Global Issues & Solutions.
<https://bwwsociety.org/journal/current/2019/jan-feb/language-as-a-living-entity.htm>

dialects are subject to two opposing processes that may influence language unity:

    a. **Repulsive Force**: This involves the continuous divergence of dialects and a decrease in mutual intelligibility due to varied social interactions and the influence of different cultures. This force weakens internal communication by fostering dialectal diversification, which, in turn, encourages sub-social identities to evolve into distinct ethnic groups with their unique cultures. Over time, major dialects like Sorani and Kurmanji may gain prominence, each becoming an ethnolect within its respective region, potentially replacing a unified Kurdish identity.

    b. **Gravitative Force**: The widespread use of modern technology, social media, and increased satellite broadcasts enhances internal communication among speakers of different dialects. This contact raises the level of mutual intelligibility and promotes linguistic and social unification. However, this process requires a unified form of language to facilitate effective inter-dialectal communication.

These contradictory forces could either propel Kurdish towards fragmentation or unification. Therefore, it is imperative to adopt a common lexicon and writing system, supported by a comprehensive language plan and effective policy, to secure the proficiency of Kurdish in the future.

3.4.1 A Language? or Independent Dialects?

As language, in general, is recognized as a human tool for exchanging data, this generic definition views it from the perspective of linguistic functionality, emphasizing its role as an innate mechanism for conveying expression among humans, irrespective of the specific language used, whether Kurdish, English, Russian, or any other set of conventional words and grammar. Indonesian Professor H. Douglas Brown (2007) defines language as:

III. Evolution of Kurdish

"a systematic means of communicating ideas or feelings by the use of conventionalized signs, sounds, gestures, or marks having understood meanings."

According to this abstract concept, language has effectively functioned as a medium for conveying simple notations and expressions among its speakers. However, the term *'language'* also covers another concept: it refers to a specific instance of a language system, such as English, French, or Urdu, among the thousands of languages that have existed.

The Swiss linguist Ferdinand de Saussure made a crucial distinction between these two meanings, referring to a specific language system as "*langue*" and the usage of that system in speech as "parole". Saussure's concept of "langue" encompasses the system of signs agreed upon by a speech community, representing an abstract structure of words and rules, akin to the English word "tongue." This structure exists independently of individual speech acts (parole). For example, in a courtroom analogy, the law represents the langue, while each verdict is a parole.

Since precision matters in certain practices of parole, the need for a clear and distinct set of norms (grammar, vocabulary, etc.), that is a single langue, is emphasized. The best a language can be is a unique set of rules and words (Lyons, 1981, p. 2), for instance, Arabic has an integral structure of grammar, syntax, and lexicon, while the Egyptian dialect shares most Arabic rules and words yet has its distinct structure, making each a different langue. However, to maintain integrity, the colloquial is used in day-to-day communication while the standard variety is solely reserved as formal.

Unlike Arabic, Kurdish lacks unified oral and orthographic unity, raising questions about whether Kurdish can be represented as a unique langue or is, instead, a set of langues. Saussure's approach to a "language" requires a single recognized dialect for formal use, whether spoken by a community or selected for high-level communication.

In a similar vein, Norwegian does not have a single formal dialect; instead, two recognized varieties, Nynorsk and Bokmål, are equally accepted as formal Norwegian. However, each variety is understood by the entire Norwegian population, fostering almost complete linguistic unity, a status not available for Kurdish speakers.

As a result of ignoring the importance of a unique standard, the tendency grew among Kurds to prefer the ease of using the local dialect at the expense of the burdensome process of coining a single, unified variety. Some linguists may argue, in addition, that the formal use of a dialect ensures a better and more accurate personal ability to express feelings and offers faster learning for children, especially in the early years of study, as it is closer to the variety used at home. This plurality suggests that Kurdish is not a language in the sense of "langue" but rather a group of langues that need to move toward a unified formulation to meet the comprehensive definition of language.

The Saussurean definition of parole focuses more on utterance as the primary concrete instance than orthographic representation. (*) Signifying utterance was comprehensible when he introduced his theory more than a century ago—that is, before the increasing practice of written communication. However, during the 1960s, office work began to flourish as cities expanded, written communication became common in business, and office work increased in the 1980s after the advent of the computer. By the turn of the twenty-first century, remote work began to spread across corporate intranets, further signifying the prominence of writing at the expense of oral use. Written communication requires a unique linguistic standard, a single langue, unlike oral communication which tolerates multiple langues.

3.5 Modification of Kurdish

For centuries, oral Kurdish sufficed for daily communication. However, due to the lack of its own orthography, Kurdish was not utilized for academic purposes, documentation, or as a scripting

---

* Klose, Robert (13 Sep. 2023). The Christian Science Monitor

III. Evolution of Kurdish

language. Writing in Kurdish was so neglected that even gravestones in Kurdish-speaking regions were inscribed in Arabic, the liturgical language. Consequently, prominent Kurdish figures were discouraged from writing their scientific, religious, and literary works in Kurdish.

It was not until the late 18th century that Kurdish began to be documented systematically. The first significant linguistic study, "*Grammatica e vocabolario della lingua Kurda*" (Grammar and Vocabulary of the Kurdish Language), was published in Rome in 1787 by the Italian Kurdologist Maurizio Garzoni (1734–1804). In the late 19th century, the initial step toward using Kurdish in publications was made by the Bedirxan brothers, who launched the journal "Kurdistan" in Cairo in 1898.

Despite these early efforts, the Kurdish did not attempt to standardize writing systems until after the collapse of the Russian Empire. The initial writing system was developed to meet the needs of publishing communist literature in Soviet Armenia. Although the outcomes were not linguistically significant following the collapse of the Republic of Red Kurdistan, they inspired later modifications by Celadet Bedirxan.

Written communication until that time was documented using the Arabic-Persian script, akin to that employed in Ottoman Turkish, Persian, and Urdu. This is evidenced by historical literary works, the Kurdistan newspaper, and the correspondence of King Mahmood. The principal linguistic modification efforts at that time were primarily directed toward the development of a new Kurdish writing system, rather than achieving lexical unity within the language.

Major advancements occurred in the 20th century with the systematization of Sorani grammar in the 1920s and Kurmanji grammar in the 1930s, driven by the political changes following World War I. These efforts successfully created writing systems but failed to establish a universal linguistic standard recognized by speakers of other Kurdish dialects. This failure deepened dialectal divisions and did not prevent the anticipated transformation of these dialects into separate forms of languages.

3.5.1 Modification of Wahbi and Bedirxan

As a result of the collapse of the Ottoman Empire, the British forces found themselves in control of a significant portion of the Kurdish-speaking regions. Consequently, there arose a need for an appropriate language for administrative purposes. Kurdish, at that time, lacked a fully developed orthographic system, and local administrations in Kurdistan were unable to communicate effectively in Arabic, the formal language of the newly established state of Iraq. The British occupation's administrative demands led to efforts to adapt Kurdish for local administrative functions.

When Colonel Tawfiq Wahbi was appointed to address this issue, he prioritized a local dialect from the Sulaymaniyah region, disregarding the concept of a nationwide intelligible linguistic standard. Due to the limited intelligibility across dialects, a decade later, Celadet Bedirxan initiated another writing system tailored for Kurmanji speakers. These orthographic projects marked a significant phase in the modernization of Kurdish. They laid the groundwork for a standard form with a defined lexicon, syntax, and grammar, enabling Kurdish to meet the needs of the following century. However, these systems also had significant drawbacks and failed to establish a cohesive and integral language.

Local Scope

The first major drawback was the low intelligibility across dialects. Each orthographic system focused on a specific geographic area, neglecting the needs of speakers in other regions. The Soviet project was based on the dialect spoken in Armenia, the Sorani resources were limited to the variety in Sulaymaniyah, and Bedirxan's efforts concentrated on Kurmanji without considering other dialects.

Phonological Base

All three initiatives aimed to create a transparent orthography, where the spelling closely reflected pronunciation, adhering to strict phonological principles. This approach aimed for maximum correspondence between phonemes and graphemes. However, this

III. Evolution of Kurdish

conservative strategy was unsuitable for a multi-dialect language like Kurdish, which exhibits a *continuum* where linguistic differences accumulate over distance. Pronunciation variations increase with geographical expansion, leading to significant changes in phonetic habits and patterns. Transparent orthography, while beneficial in some contexts, proved ineffective for Kurdish. Conversely, an opaque orthography (see section 6.2.4) would have been adaptable to wider linguistic variation, accommodating the diverse dialectal structures, and suitable for the majority of speakers.

Negligence of History

Pronunciation of words evolves over generations and varies by region, increasing morpheme bias over time. Adopting the prevailing pronunciation of a specific period in a particular region without considering diachronic and regional differences undermines the true sound of words, making the lexicon seem strange to speakers in other regions. The efforts to compile words from villagers, derive rules and coin new terms means neglecting the diachronic bias where the common root of a morpheme may suit more dialectal variations. The scarcity of logistical resources, historical and linguistic research, and insufficient studies on the Pahlavi language, from which much of the Kurdish vocabulary is derived, further complicated Wahbi-Bedirxan efforts.

In summary, while the initial orthographic projects in the 20th century revolutionized the use of Kurdish and enabled it to meet modern requirements, they were limited by their focus on the local dialect, phonological conservatism, and the negligence of historical social transformations. These limitations hindered the establishment of a universal Kurdish linguistic standard, perpetuating dialectal divisions and impeding the development of a unified language.

3.5.2 Second Phase of Modification

The methods and achievements adopted by I. Marogulov (and A. Shamo), T. Wahbi (based on S. Kaban), and C. Bedirxan are, although had revolutionized the use of Kurdish at the beginning of the 20th century, from a contemporary perspective, outdated and insufficient to meet current social and political demands, and even less so for future requirements. The substantial social developments throughout the second half of the 20th century and the first quarter of the 21st necessitate further initiatives to complete the process of linguistic revival. This entails a second phase to achieve the target, incorporating the following measures:

    a. **Language Ideology**: To enhance the social status and prestige of Kurdish among native speakers, expand its use at the expense of neighboring formal languages, and address the social gaps that attract modern sociolinguistic patterns. This may involve promoting the acceptance of modified standardization, encouraging monolingualism within Kurdish society, and creating a linguistic strategy for deploying a purified and unified variety (see Chapter 5).

    b. **Language Planning**: To implement linguistic reforms such as reviving morphological roots, extracting efficient affixes, and coining new words. In addition to corpus planning, status planning is necessary to promote language prestige, and acquisition planning to facilitate learning (see Section 5.2).

    c. **Language Policy**: To establish rules and regulations that enable practical and legal means for deploying unified standards and enhancing the functions of Kurdish within speaker communities (see Section 5.3).

The process of language promotion and linguistic modification should be managed by an accredited linguistic body in the form of an authorized academy. Such a body would formulate plans, provide technical proposals, and collaborate with relevant departments to ensure the effective implementation of these measures.

IV. A Language Is a Nation

"Tell me how much a nation knows about its own language, and I will tell you how much that nation knows about its own identity."

John Ciardi

Apart from being a primary means of communication, language's underlying capabilities significantly impact social interaction by shaping thoughts and perceptions. According to the linguistic relativity hypothesis proposed by Edward Sapir and Benjamin Lee Whorf, known as the Sapir-Whorf hypothesis, languages exhibit variations in the conceptualization of thoughts, thereby a particular language influences the way reality is conceived instinctively and is dissimilar to ways influenced by other human languages. This linguistic distinctiveness plays a pivotal role in shaping various social perceptions, encompassing cultural, political, and psychological dimensions within society. (Whorf, 1956, p. 147)

Also, differing lifestyles, such as nomadic and settled, contribute unique attitudes and values to a culture. Nomadic societies may foster a sense of tribal unity, self-sacrifice for communal interests, reverence for ancestors, and gender-specific attitudes. Conversely, settled populations may exhibit higher tolerance for individualism, intellectual pluralism, and a propensity for peaceful coexistence. These socio-cultural traits, originating from environmental factors, are ingrained in language through epics, myths, proverbs, religious texts, and literature. Such historical literary expressions are inherited and continue to influence contemporary lifestyles, permeating mass media, educational curricula, and societal emotions.

The language spoken by a community profoundly influences its cultural orientation. For instance, Kurds speaking Arabic may absorb prevalent Arab cultural norms, while those speaking Persian may align with Iranian cultural practices, potentially diverging from their Kurdish heritage and failing to meet local social needs adequately. Thus a unique national language consolidates cultural unity. Alesina, Giuliano, and Reich view the national language as a pivotal instrument in nation-building, which entails fostering a shared national identity among citizens. (2018, p. 2) adding that nation-building involves creating a sense of commonality in interests, goals, and preferences among citizens, thus preventing fragmentation and promoting national cohesion:

> *"We define 'nation-building' as a process which leads to the formation of countries in which the citizens feel a sufficient amount of commonality of interests, goals, and preferences that they do not wish to separate from each other."*

Today, there are around seven thousand living languages in the world; each is a treasury of knowledge and culture that has been created throughout the ages as a result of the suffering and experiences of each nation. Half of these living languages are believed to be extinct in the next hundred years. That is at the rate of one language dying every week! Each time a language dies, a nation is moved from geography to history.

In conclusion, the vitality of a nation is intricately linked to the preservation of its language. The death of a language signifies not only the loss of linguistic diversity but also the erosion of a nation's cultural identity and historical significance.

The dissolution of nations often stems from neglecting the intrinsic value of linguistic and cultural heritage, leaving them vulnerable to collapse, as Renan (1882/1992, para III) aptly noted:

> *"The secession and, in the long run, collapse of nations are the consequence of a system which placed these old organisms at the mercy of often poorly enlightened wills."*

IV. A Language Is a Nation

4.1 Nationalism

Since each language conceptualizes terms and influences cultures based on inherited environmental and historical events, the concept of 'Nation' varies from one culture to the next, depending on the sociocultural heritage too. The Western definition of a nation often emphasizes political dimensions, whereas nomadic cultures such as Arabic and Turkish define the term based on ancestral lineage and racial origins. In contrast, the Iranian concept of a nation tends to focus on territorial affinity. This divergence in definitions creates diverse and sometimes mystical perspectives on the notion of a nation in general, and Kurdish identity in particular. Kurds, dispersed across international borders, define their identity according to regional influences and the conceptual frameworks of neighboring cultures. For instance, in the Iranian part of the Kurdish-speaking region, nationality is predominantly influenced by linguistic specificity. Conversely, for Kurds within Turkey's borders, language is not the primary factor in defining their national identity.

4.1.1 Racial Cultures

In cultures that have inherited a desert nomadic or semi-nomadic lifestyle, where population groups may travel to find food or pasture for livestock, adapting less emotional connection to a specific land, tribal hierarchical descent represents the ultimate identity through the family tree. Nationality, therefore, is uniquely racial, specified irrespective of the region of settlement or citizenship documents. This definition is exemplified in Arab and Turkish cultural models. For instance, an Arab person's nationality remains the same, and a Turk remains a Turk, regardless of how many generations have settled in a foreign land, the language spoken, or the documents held. Conversely, a non-Arab family would never be deemed Arab, no matter how long they have lived within Arab society or how extensively they have adopted its language and cultural concepts. Moreover, an Arab in Iraq shares the same national identity as any other Arab from Syria, Egypt, Morocco, Brazil, or any person believed to be a descendant of an Arab tribe. This definition is supported by mythological explanations that trace the nation's roots back to a single progenitor, the great patriarch of the nation. Since ethnic identity is based on unique and pure paternal kinship, a person cannot change or acquire a second nationality.

Based on this notion, until the early twentieth century, Arabs of North Africa and the Nile basin were not considered part of the Arab nation, as it was believed that these Arabic-speaking populations were not originally descendants of the Arab race. The first nationalist Arab movement, "*Le réveil de la nation arabe*", founded in Paris by Nagib Azouri in December 1904, stated in its manifesto published a month later that the homeland of the Arabs extends from the Mesopotamia Valley in the east to the Gulf of Suez in the west, and from the Mediterranean Sea in the north to the Sea of Oman in the south. (*) (Azouri, 1905, p. 6, 37)

4.1.2 Territorial Cultures

Typically, a settled society defines the nation as the entire population that shares homeland resources and adopts cultural norms regardless of language or racial descendency. This definition is evident in the Iranian culture in such a way that a family of an Iranian-born generation holds Iranian nationality regardless of race or language as long as it shares what is phrased as 'water and land' (آب و خاک). Generally, race and linguistic characteristics declined to a lower status than the territorial and sociocultural norms. According to this definition, an Iranian of Persian descent does not share the nationality with other Persians in Afghanistan and Tajikistan, rather, shares with Iranian compatriots no matter what their race or mother tongue is, such as Arabs, Kurds, Azeries, and Baluches. A person who lives abroad may gain a second nationality; however, his first is preserved as his roots. Overall, religious doctrine (as a prominent part of culture) enjoys higher significance than race and linguistic

---

* The source text:
"وسوف تمتد حدود هذه الامبراطورية العربية الجديدة حدودها الطبيعية من وادي دجلة والفرات حتى برزخ السويس، ومن البحر الابيض المتوسط حتى بحر عمان"

variation. Nonetheless, specific cultural traits of these minorities may reject territorial affinities, prioritizing the racial bonds across borders, or separatism.

This definition complies with what Ernest Renan (1882/1992, para V) described. He defined the 'nation' as a spiritual principle where race, language, interests, religious affinity, geography, or military necessities alone would not suffice to create but rather a composition of all with variable magnitudes. However, he stressed that a nation evolves mainly due to geographical factors throughout history:

> "Geography is one of the essential factors in history. Rivers have distributed the races; mountains have stopped them. The former encouraged whereas the latter discouraged the great historical movements."

4.1.3 Cultures of Citizenship

The European revolutions fundamentally reshaped traditional ideas, laying the groundwork for modern concepts that became entrenched in the latter half of the 20th century. A significant example of this transformation in modern perspectives, individuals are no longer assessed based on religion, race, or language; instead, equal rights codified in legal documents become the primary measure of national identity. This principle, especially prevalent in Western culture, considers nationality primarily as a matter of legal citizenship. Upon obtaining the right to permanent residency, an individual is considered a member of the nation, irrespective of ethnicity, religion, or place of birth. In addition, individuals may hold multiple nationalities as permitted by specific national laws. Consequently, ethnicity, religion, and race are no longer valid criteria for national belonging.

However, culturally and socially distinct groups that cannot form independent political/administrative entities are not recognized as nations but are classified as ethnic groups without legitimate rights to pursue independence. For instance, the Kurdish populations in Turkey and Iran are limited to advocating for cultural recognition and promotion. Independence movements within these groups are often deemed rebellions against legitimate authority and the sovereign country, and if coupled with armed struggle, they are typically labeled as terrorist activities.

A recognized self-governing group can be designated as a "stateless nation." If such a group gains official recognition of its territorial boundaries, entities like the Iraqi Kurdistan Region and the administration of Northern Syria could qualify as stateless nations with subsequent, and limited, privileges to seek independence.

4.1.3.1 Stateless Nations

Similar to the definition of "Nation," the political term "State" is also subject to various interpretations. However, it primarily denotes a "political entity with an independent or semi-independent territorial system construct." This term can sometimes refer to an independent country and, at other times, to a federal division within a country, such as the states in the United States of America.

Benedict Anderson (1991, pp. 6-7) expanded the concept of the state by developing the notion of an imagined community, describing a nation as a socially constructed community that may also manifest in non-sovereign states:

> *"an imagined political community—and imagined as both inherently limited and sovereign."*

The definition of a stateless nation is concluded as *a nation without territorial sovereignty,* and stateless nations as the *fourth world.*

Despite the distinct cultural and social identity of the Kurds within Turkey, the recognition of a Kurdish nation within Turkish borders remains ambiguous. Kurds possess a unique socio-cultural identity and express clear political aspirations, however, they have not yet established a form of self-administration that meets Western standards for nationhood. Consequently, Turkish authorities oppose official recognition of the Kurds to prevent the emergence of a recognized stateless nation according to Western criteria. It may peacefully advocate for independence, whereas ethnic groups without national status are often denied such recognition and support by the West.

4.2 Language & Nationalism

Historically, there have been numerous examples of the strong connection between language and national identity. In modern Western Europe, during the Nazi occupation of France, the French language was banned as part of the Germanization campaigns. Similarly, the French authorities implemented restrictive linguistic policies to counter Algerian nationalism. Ironically, post-independence Arab Algeria employed similar measures against the burgeoning national aspirations of the Amazigh minority.

Repressed nations strive to promote their languages, while central governments aim to suppress these languages to curb the emergence of distinct national identities. In ethnocratic states, language also becomes the primary criterion for first-class citizenship, symbolizing ethnic identity. Consequently, ethnic purification policies implemented by central governments frequently restrict the use of minority languages. In other ethnocratic states such as Turkey, Syria, and Baathist Iraq, these languages were banned or systematically oppressed to prevent the development of political national entities. Also, despite the ethnic impartiality claimed by theological standards, Iran continues to ban ethnic languages in education, as they could fuel nationalism, which contradicts the ideology of the clerical doctrine.

The suppression of minority languages and their systematic marginalization aim to diminish the national character of ethnic groups. This structured policy underscores the fact that language is a potent factor in defining nationality and serves as a political representative of ethnic rights movements.

Since language serves as a distinct marker of national identity and has consistently played a crucial role in nationalist conflicts, particularly in the Middle East, it has been used as an authenticating proof in claiming disputed territories. The right to claim a landscape is typically evaluated based on its historical authenticity, which is determined by the presence of the language within antiquities and the broader cultural heritage.

4.2.1 Symbol of Ethnicity

Isolated tribes develop their sociocultural systems in tandem with distinctive linguistic characteristics. When a particular tribal dialect evolves into a fully-fledged language, the tribe transforms into a distinct ethnicity, cultivating a stereotyped social character. Individuals assimilate into shared cultural traits that overshadow the specifics of social classes. Language thus becomes an ethnic symbol, often intertwined with emotions and politically leveraged as an identity marker for ultra-nationalist movements and religious orientations.

"*Speak, so that I may see where you are from.*" (*) This interpretation of one of Socrates's famous quotations underscores the significance of language as the foremost means of transferring thoughts among individuals. It is also a common practice to discern an individual's origin based on their native language, with dialect and accent providing more specific details. Moreover, language or dialect can indicate social class and typical behavior. Examples of sociolinguistic identity include the sociolect *African American Vernacular English* (AAVE) spoken by working-class Americans of African origin, the Cockney accent of London's eastern suburbs, Turkic Azeri in Tehran, and the dialect of the Al-Sadr suburb in Baghdad that is influenced by the Southern Iraq Arabic dialect.

The role of one's linguistic pattern is decisive in revealing their background and social status. Consequently, individuals who seek to switch ethnic identities or social classes and assimilate into another (higher prestige) group often adopt the linguistic behavior of that group.

---

* A quote from Socrates says "Speak, so that I may see you."

4.3 Bilingualism

Bilingualism is the ability of an individual or a community to use two languages fluently. This phenomenon can be seen in various degrees, from individuals who have near-native proficiency in both languages to those who can manage simple conversations in a second while being fluent in their primary language.

The vast majority of the Kurdish population is known for its bilingual structure. Along with Kurdish, the mother tongue of the majority, Turkish in the north, Arabic in the south, and Persian in the east are second languages that have attained popularity during the twentieth century with the support of the states and as a result of assimilation policies. Yet, Kurdish does not share the same popularity as the formal language due to its nature of utilization; while it is used mainly for oral and domestic communication, the other languages are imposed on administrative and educational use. This has led to deploying Kurdish at a different rate between the countryside, which is considered the linguistic mine of the language, and the major cities, where the linguistic assimilation intensified and Kurdish faces the threat of losing dominance or even disappearance.

4.3.1 Linguistic Acquisitions

Often individuals acquire their mother tongues at home first, then other languages at different ages in their lives. However, more than one language may be acquired simultaneously as in multilingual societies like the large Kurdish cities in Iran and Turkey. Learning is classified into three types: *co-ordinate*, *compound*, and *subordinate*.

4.3.1.1 Compound

The concept of compound learning refers to the simultaneous acquisition of two languages within the same household, typically resulting from a mixed-culture family environment or when both languages hold comparable levels of prevalence and fluency. This form of bilingualism is frequently observed among the large Kurdish communities (Kurdish quarters) in non-Kurdish towns, in bilingual marriages, and in large multilingual cities such as Kirkuk and Kermanshah. It is also prevalent in regions where state languages dominate urban areas, such as Afrin, Amed, and Mahabad, where Kurdish is not permitted in educational settings.

The pervasive use of the state language in these contexts poses a significant threat to the status of Kurdish, potentially leading to its decline in everyday market communication.

4.3.1.2 Co-ordinate

A child typically acquires their mother tongue at home and subsequently learns a second language later, primarily through schooling. This sequential learning process is common among Kurdish diasporas worldwide, where parents often do not speak the dominant languages at home. It is also prevalent in smaller Kurdish towns and rural areas, where Kurdish is excluded from the educational curriculum, necessitating the acquisition of the state language for academic purposes.

4.3.1.3 Subordinate

Subordinate language acquisition is a form of bilingualism where the second language is often learned in later stages of life through the filter of the first language. This means that the learner processes the second language (L2) using the cognitive and linguistic framework established by their first language (L1) which continues to be dominant. In this process, the learner tends to translate L2 concepts into L1 to understand and produce L2. This reliance on the first language can influence pronunciation, grammar, and usage of the second language. Late second language learning is more common in the countryside and rural areas, where the need for the state language or the dominant variety is not as urgent as it is in cities. It is also common for older people or those who did not attend formal education.

4.3.2 Language Fluency

In a multilingual society, the level of fluency in a given language significantly influences one's sense of identity. For Kurds, fluency in the Kurdish language is particularly vital as it often serves as a measure of ethnic purity. In some regions and among certain social classes, proficiency in Kurdish is considered a marker of authentic Kurdish identity. Consequently, the more fluent an individual is in Kurdish, the more their originality and cultural authenticity are recognized. This concept of purism links the degree of Kurdishness directly to one's dialect and fluency level.

4.3.2.1 Mother Tongue

The lullabies sung by Kurdish mothers, often among the first words a Kurdish child hears, typically establish the mother tongue. However, for a Kurdish child, this is not always the case, especially in recent decades. In modern urban settings within Kurdish regions, as well as in the diaspora, many Kurdish mothers themselves are not fluent. Consequently, some Kurdish children grow up with a different mother tongue. This phenomenon is evident among numerous Kurds residing in various parts of Northern Kurdistan, as well as among Kurdish families settled in southern Iraq, western Turkey, Syria, and Europe.

4.3.2.2 Native Language

The native language is the language predominantly used in a community, such as in the town center, market, school, or among the majority of friends. It can differ from the mother tongue, especially in multilingual urban areas. This phenomenon is rapidly becoming common worldwide, not just among Kurds in the diaspora, but also in places like Kirkuk, Gaziantep, and Urmia, as well as in cities with Kurdish minorities. The Kurdish population is notably bilingual, with a significant portion speaking a native language different from their mother tongue. However, in monolingual societies, the mother tongue and the native language typically coincide.

4.3.2.3 Language of Origin

Over time, the process of assimilation can lead to a gradual shift from one language to another. This transition may ultimately result in a group abandoning their ancestral language in favor of a new one. Language shifts can occur voluntarily, as seen in countries with high levels of immigration such as the United States, Australia, and Russia's Siberia. Alternatively, they can be imposed through forceful assimilation policies, as observed in Kurdistan, Indonesia, and Sri Lanka. Currently, a large portion of the Kurdish population in Turkey (reliable statistics are unavailable) is considered monolingual, communicating solely in Turkish, which is now regarded as their mother tongue despite it not being the language of their forebears. This situation is similarly observed in Syria and southern Iraq, where Kurdish has been eliminated from daily communication both within and outside the home.

Therefore, the language of origin, which pertains to the previous generation, still signifies the linguistic roots of a populace. Consequently, Kurds who have lost the ability to use Kurdish for communication are still considered to have Kurdish as their language of origin, even if they are no longer able to speak it.

4.3.2.4 Most Fluent Language

In most parts of the world, particularly in modern Western societies, each indigenous group enjoys the right to linguistic practice as part of their legally protected liberties. The state permits the free use of the mother tongue in public and formally in written communication. The dominant mother tongue is almost always the native language of the community, leading to the frequent conflation of the terms *'mother tongue'* and *'native language'* in linguistic studies. However, the assimilation policies are still common elsewhere. In Kurdistan, for instance, assimilation has historically compelled Kurdish speakers to keep their mother tongue at home, necessitating the use of different languages in other contexts. This often results in issues with fluency in Kurdish.

The balance of languages shows that if the mother tongue is more influential than the state language, young students are discouraged from educational progress, and suffer negative psychological effects. Conversely, if the language of education is perceived to dominate the mother tongue, educated individuals may become disconnected from their language of origin and local cultures.

The phenomenon of enforcing state languages for literature is an old tradition that has intensified significantly in the last century. The superiority of the native language over the mother tongue has led to greater proficiency; as a result, prominent figures such as Yashar Kemal (Nobel Prize nominee), Suzan Samanci, and Yavuz Ekinci wrote their literary masterpieces in Turkish; Saleem Barakat, Marouf Al-Rasafi, and Al-Zahawi in Arabic; and Lari Kermanshahi, Moeini Kermanshahi, and Muhammad Ali Afghan in Persian. Although their works touched on Kurdish social life, such as poverty, racism, and ruthless tribal traditions, they expressed their experiences in languages unfamiliar to their culture of origin.

This linguistic shift has led to a gradual erosion of the mother tongue's status, cutting off cultural roots and exposing Kurdish intellectuals to state political influences and propaganda. Consequently, some Kurds have participated in anti-Kurd activities; for instance, Diyarbakir-born Ziya Gökalp was a key architect of the Turkification policies of Kemalist pan-Turkism.

Fluency in a language significantly influences various social fields and is an effective factor in political orientation. A language with a high level of fluency shapes the self-identification of individuals, thereby affecting the identity of the entire community. Thus, when a group of Kurds who are more fluent in Turkish begins to identify as Turks, the community is perceived as Turkish rather than Kurdish.

4.4 Constitutional Recognition

According to the Ethnologue Research Center, there were 7,151 living languages worldwide in 2022. The vast majority of these languages are not officially recognized by the constitutions of 195 existing countries. Some designate a single language as the sole official, such as Turkey, Iran, and Syria, while others recognize multiple languages as constitutionally official, including Iraq, Afghanistan, and India. Additionally, it is common for some countries to refrain from specifying any official language, such as the United Kingdom and Australia. Despite the fact that English is the predominant spoken language in the United States, it is noteworthy that English is not designated as the official language of the country and functions only as a de facto national language.

4.4.1 The National Language

The native language spoken by the majority of people and functioning as the de facto language of the nation, regardless of its official status, is referred to as the *national language*. Given the ambiguous definition of the term '*nation*', the concept of a 'national language' is similarly vague. Typically, it denotes the primary language of the majority within a country, such as Turkish in Turkey, where it is the only officially recognized national language. Alternatively, if the concept of nation includes every distinct sociocultural entity, the Kurds qualify as a nation within the borders of the Turkish Republic. Consequently, Kurdish, alongside Turkish, can be considered a national language due to its significant proportion of speakers. However, political motives influence this concept; thus, since Turkish authorities do not promote the use of Kurdish (and other local languages) in public domains, non of them is recognized as a national language. In contrast, countries with broader liberties acknowledge multiple national languages, such as Spain, South Africa, and Canada.

4.4.2 Official Languages

The language designated for administrative purposes such as judiciary, trade, and the education system, regardless of whether it is the native language of the nation, is termed the official language. This designation can be established by the state either constitutionally, thus gaining "de jure" status (official by law), or through widespread

IV. A Language Is a Nation

use and recognition without formal legal endorsement, thereby existing as "de facto" (official in practice but not by legal right).

For instance, de jure official languages include Kurdish, which is officially recognized in Iraq; Turkish, in Turkey and Cyprus; and Persian, in Iran, Afghanistan, and Tajikistan (with names of Farsi, Dari, and Tajik). These languages are explicitly mentioned in the constitutions of these countries. Conversely, some nations do not constitutionally declare an official language but recognize their national languages as de facto official. Examples include Spanish in Mexico and Costa Rica, and English in the United Kingdom, the United States, and Australia. Notably, Italian was constitutionally designated as official only in March 2007, thus achieving de jure status. (*)

Additionally, some countries recognize multiple official languages. For example, Iraq recognizes both Arabic and Kurdish, Luxembourg acknowledges Luxembourgish, German, and French, and Switzerland has four official languages. The countries with the highest number of official languages include:

	Country	Official Languages
1	Bolivia	37
2	India	23
3	Zimbabwe	16
4	South Africa	11
5	Switzerland	4
6	Singapore	4
7	Rwanda	4

Another model followed by multilingual countries involves recognizing a single national official language while allowing local

---

* https://www.reuters.com/article/oukoe-uk-italy-language-idUKL3041879820070330

languages to have official status within specific administrative divisions. For instance, Russia officially recognizes the Russian language as the sole official for the country, nonetheless grants official status to 35 minority languages in various territorial divisions. In multilingual societies where no single native *Endoglossic* language achieves broad intelligibility or consensus, a non-native (*Exoglossic*) language is chosen. This exoglossic official language, known as a *lingua franca*, includes examples like English in India, Singapore, and Nigeria. Although not officially recognized in native-speaking countries like the United Kingdom, the United States, and Australia (where it is considered de facto), English serves as the de jure official in over sixty countries across all continents such as Canada, Nigeria, and Ghana, in addition to other countries where it is not the primary language such as India, Malta, and Pakistan.

4.4.3 Language of Stateless Nations

The recognition of a language as a primary symbol to represent national identity has led states to exert substantial pressure on the languages of stateless nations within their borders. Such state oppression strategically aims to weaken the identities of ethnic minorities by impeding their linguistic development.

A traditional method of linguistic suppression involves the displacement of speakers to geographically distant areas. Within the Kurdish-speaking region, tribal displacement has been historically implemented as follows:

Iran: During the Safavid Empire under Shah Abbas, significant displacement of Kurdish speakers was enforced. The major destination was to the far most point from their homeland (the northeast region of *Khurasan*) bordering Afghanistan and Turkmenistan.

Turkey: The Turkish Republic, building on legislation from the era of Sultan Muhammad Rashad the Fifth, enforced Kurdish displacement laws. Additionally, policies during the Turkish Republic period aimed at impoverishing Kurdish-speaking regions to encourage permanent voluntary migration from the region. (Bedirxan, 2011)

Syria: Following the 1962 census, the 'Arab Belt' policy (1965-1976) displaced Kurds from their lands, replacing them with Arab tribes. (*)

Iraq: Under the monarchy, Kurdish populations were evacuated from areas such as Kirkuk and Hawija in an early stage of Arabization. The campaign continued under the Republic regimes, especially in the seventies and eighties. Following an ultra-nationalist ideology, during the rule of the Baath party, forced displacement and linguistic assimilation dramatically intensified. Thousands of Kurdish villages were destroyed and millions of people were displaced within Iraq or deported across the Iranian borders.

Turkish assimilation campaign

The strategy of stripping a nation of its linguistic roots manifests in various ways. Currently, Turkish authorities employ the following methods to undermine the Kurdish language:

1. **Disunion**: The plan involves emphasizing linguistic variations by exaggerating dialect differences, thereby aggravating intelligibility issues in cross-dialect communication. This practice encourages speakers to use the state language as a lingua franca instead of Kurdish varieties, ultimately preventing Kurdish from sustaining its sociocultural characteristics as a unified, distinct national identity.

2. **Stagnation**: Efforts are made to prevent Kurdish from evolving into a modern urban language, preventing it from containing contemporary social changes, developing modern vocabulary, and updating patterns and expressions. Without these updates, Kurdish fails to meet social interests in fields like art, fashion, and sports,

---

* Nicolas A. Heras, The Battle for Syria's Al-Hasakah Province, Combating Terrorism Center, volume 6, issue 10

stigmatizing the language as a primitive rural, degrading its prestige to the lowest level (substratum), and inhibiting its growth and modernization.

4.4.4 Minority Languages

The number of nations around the world is countable, as referenced by the United Nations statistics, however, due to the varying definitions of the term "*minority*", the overall number of minorities is vague. There are several interpretations of the term. The UN, aligning with human rights perspectives, defines a minority as:

> *"An ethnic, religious or linguistic minority is any group of persons which constitutes less than half of the population in the entire territory of a State whose members share common characteristics of culture, religion or language, or a combination of any of these."* (*)

Although this definition overlooks that many majority groups worldwide also constitute less than half of the population, the UN does not classify them as minorities based on equality requirements; instead, their relative numerical advantage grants them privileges that officialize their superiority.

According to international standards, a populace is considered a nation only if it resides within a state with defined borders and has international recognition. This notion is shaped by historical outcomes of wars, where borders were drawn, often arbitrarily, leading to a distribution of populations that does not always align with ethnic or cultural boundaries. Consequently, minorities arise more as a byproduct of these historical conflicts than from adherence to human rights principles.

Under the United Nations definition, the Kurds are not recognized as a nation but are instead categorized mainly as distinct minorities

---

* Office of the High Commissioner of Human Rights
https://www.ohchr.org/en/special-procedures/sr-minority-issues/concept-minority-mandate-definition

IV. A Language Is a Nation

dispersed across Turkey, Syria, Iraq, and Iran, in addition to smaller communities.

However, in many multi-ethnic states, the largest ethnic group may not constitute a majority of the population. In some cases, a numerically smaller group may hold significant political power, as seen in Ethiopia. The Amhara, although a numerical minority, wield considerable influence, while the larger Oromo population is considered a minority.

The ethnic composition of Ethiopia is as follows:

1	Oromo	33.8 %
2	Amhara	29.3 %
3	Somali	6.2 %
4	Tigrinya	5.9 %
5	Sidamo	4.0 %

The top five languages in Ethiopia (2007 census). (*)

Despite the relatively low numerical representation, the Amharic language holds a dominant position as the primary language of administration and education. In other parts of the world, a minority group can achieve formal recognition regardless of its population size. For instance, in Switzerland, the Romansh minority, which comprises only 0.5% (approximately 40,000 individuals) of the nation's 8.7 million population, enjoys official recognition similar to the German-speaking majority which comprises 63%. (†)

4.4.4.1 Linguistic Discrimination

In many states, particularly in the developing world, when minorities face persecution, their languages are also subjected to systematic denial. Ethnic repression is invariably accompanied by

---

* Ethnic Group and Mother Tongue in the Ethiopian Censuses of 1994 and 2007, ISSN 2194–4024
† Federal Statistical Office, Switzerland, 2022

linguistic discrimination, making the term 'racism' synonymous with 'linguicism'. For instance, in Turkey, the Kurdish ethnicity, along with Arabs, Laz, and Circassians, is not officially recognized as a minority despite these groups being estimated to constitute 30% of the country's population. According to the Lausanne Treaty of 1923, the term 'minority' in Turkey applies only to non-Muslim religious groups, specifically Christians (Greek and Armenian) and Jews. Nevertheless, while the treaty's articles 38 and 39 guaranteed the right to use languages other than Turkish, (*) the Turkish Republic, based on its own definition of the term, has not upheld these provisions.

4.5 Role of Religion

Religious texts are often crafted in a carefully constructed language, rhetorically enabled to match more than a single interpretation, where any attempt to reorder or translate can distort their meaning, reduce their sanctity, or make them subject to debate. Consequently, religious authorities often preserve the liturgical language and advise against linguistic modifications. Despite the diversity of colloquial forms, formal Arabic, for example, has retained its linguistic rules for 14 centuries without significant changes, largely due to the influence of Islam; the religion has elevated the status of Arabic by utilizing it to convey its religious doctrines.

---

* Lausanne Treaty; in Article 38 comes:
"The Turkish Government undertakes to assure full and complete protection of life and liberty to all inhabitants of Turkey without distinction of birth, nationality, language, race or religion."

In article 39 comes:
"No restrictions shall be imposed on the free use by any Turkish national of any language in private intercourse, in commerce, religion, in the press, or in publications of any kind or at public meetings.

Notwithstanding the existence of the official language, adequate facilities shall be given to Turkish nationals of non-Turkish speech for the oral use of their own language before the Courts."

IV. A Language Is a Nation

Similarly, Judaism revived the dead Hebrew almost a century ago, thereby uniting Jewish communities and reinforcing the state of Israel. Christianity, also, maintained Latin until the decline of church dominance, and Latin served as a repository for Catholic theological discourse. When a language is intertwined with religious beliefs, it provides a framework for religious teachings, and in turn, the religion helps preserve and elevate the language. This symbiotic relationship ensures the language's longevity and unity.

The power of a liturgical language can also encompass and influence other languages. Arabic, for instance, absorbed and transformed the Semitic languages around the Arabian Peninsula, integrating and assimilating them into its structure (digested the languages and Arabized their speakers) while also heavily influencing languages like Persian, Urdu, and Turkish, which adopted significant amounts of Arabic vocabulary. Kurdish, despite its historical purity and oral tradition, did not achieve the same formal status, partly because of the sanctity attributed to Arabic in Kurdish Muslim societies, where formal language use was reserved for Arabic.

The relationship between language and religion can also be observed in other cultures, such as the Armenian language with the Armenian church and the Aramaic language with Christian communities in Mesopotamia and the Levant (Nestorian, Chaldean, and Syriac). Conversely, the decline of a religion can lead to the decline or extinction of its associated language. For instance, the fall of Zoroastrianism in the seventh century led to the fragmentation of Pahlavi into various new Iranic-based languages, and the decline of Latin followed the diminishing influence of the Catholic Church in the eighteenth century.

A language supported by religion often achieves a superstratum status beyond its native speakers. Arabic, for example, despite not being a major spoken language, is official in Somalia, Djibouti, Comoros, Chad, and Zanzibar, and holds de facto status in Eritrea and religious significance in Iran.

Had Kurdish been associated with a dominant religion within Kurdish society, it might have developed a formal writing system and documented literature comparable to Armenian, Georgian, and Aramaic. The affiliation with Kurdish religions such as Yazidism,

Zoroastrianism, Yarsanism, and Alawism provides the Kurdish language with cultural and spiritual support, potentially enhancing its status and sanctity.

4.5.1 Language, Religion & Nationalism

In addition to consolidating collective consciousness, religion regulates social norms and unites the population with sacred sentiments. These ties influence political attitudes in modern society and foster national unity and solidarity. For example, the Jewish diaspora, spread across the globe and speaking a variety of languages, would not have coalesced into a unified mainstream without the religious concept of the Promised Land and the sanctity of Hebrew. The revival of the ancient Hebrew language by the Russian Jewish linguist Eliezer Ben-Yehuda in the early 20th century symbolized the rebirth of the Jewish nation, ultimately facilitating the establishment of an independent homeland. Similarly, although many pioneer figures of Arab nationalism were Christians, they embraced Islam as an intellectual nationalist tool to maintain the alliance between religion and nationalism. Michel Aflaq, the founder of the ultranationalist Arab Socialist Resurrection Party (Al-Baath), was a Greek Orthodox Christian who was identified as a secularist. Nonetheless, he acknowledged the unifying power of Islam (Aflaq, p. 108). He wrote:

"Thus Islam evolves, a giant stride occurs in the life souls of the Arabs. The values were no longer derived from the masses of the people, nor imposed by the individuals. It stems from a superior position that rises above the people and the individuals, this assures the liberties of the individuals and harmonizes with the masses at the same time. Early Islam's era represents the unity of the Arab soul with fate, not as ignored as was, thus, its will became the will of destiny. After the spatial isolation and time of loneliness, the entire world, even the universe with all that is visible and invisible became a stage for this unity's activities to

IV. A Language Is a Nation

implement these modern values that appeared in the Arab life."
(*)

Conversely, despite the dominance of the Turkish language for many centuries during the Ottoman Empire, no enduring cultural remnants have survived from that extensive colonial heritage. This lack of lasting influence can be attributed to the absence of harmony between language and religion. Consequently, the nation rapidly contracted geographically following its defeat in World War I, effectively squandering six centuries of colonial power in the region. This phenomenon is also observed in modern Iran, where the Persian language, lacking religious support, has thus far failed to significantly influence provincial communication within the country.

Religion has the power to unify a language, and this linguistic unity, in turn, fortifies the nation. This triple alliance underscores the crucial role that the unity of religion and language plays in bolstering nationalism. Given this symbiotic relationship among language, religion, and nationalism, one can imagine a different political and linguistic landscape in the Kurdish region if Zoroastrianism, or any historically significant Kurdish religion such as Yazidism or Yarsanism, had remained dominant and Pahlavi had been the language of today's extensive Kurdish population. This reality highlights one of the primary reasons for the failure to establish a cohesive and sustainable Kurdish nation: the absence of a language aligned with a distinct religion or common doctrine. The Kurdish nation requires a language that is firmly grounded, and the Kurdish language needs the support of religion to thrive.

---

* "ثم يظهر الاسلام فيحدث انقلابا في حياة العرب وفي انفسهم. فالقيم لم تعد تستمد من المجموع، كما ان الفرد ليس هو الذي يفرضها. انها تصدر من مكان هو فوق المجموع والفرد معا، وفي هذا ضمان لحرية الفرد وانسجامه مع المجموع في آن واحد. أما صدر الاسلام فانه من ناحية اخرى يمثل اتحاد النفس العربية مع القدر بعد ان كانت متجاهلة له، لا بل الكون وكل ما هو منظور وغير منظور، مسرحا لنشاطه ولتطبيق هذه القيم الجديدية التي ظهرت في الحياة العربية."

4.6 Evolution of Sub-Nations

"*Are you a Barzani or a Talabani?*" This question has been posed to me countless times during and after the PDK-PUK conflict in May 1994, typically during casual conversations or encounters with curious strangers, often Turkish, in cafes or on long train journeys. Whenever I responded with "neither," it elicited an astonished and seemingly innocent reaction, implying another unspoken question:

"*How is that possible?*"

The reaction (second question) revealed that the primary motivation behind such an indirect inquiry was not political, as politics encompasses a wide range of orientations. Rather, the binary nature of the cause was more rooted in geographical and sociocultural distinctions. It sought to ascertain whether I identified with the Sorani or Bahdinani background, each representing distinct sub-national identities with their own cultural and social implications. This indicates that cultural variations, expressed through accent and dialect, significantly influence identity and are reflected in political alignments. The question would not have been framed in this manner if dialectal differences had not played a crucial role in shaping identities and were not perceived as a factor in defining sub-national affiliations.

4.6.1 The Russian-Ukrainian Conflict

In late February 2022, when Russian tanks crossed the Ukrainian border, followed by one of the most virally spreading questions on the internet was "*What is the difference between Russians and Ukrainians?*" This question arose from the close cultural and linguistic ties between the two neighboring nations. The underlying curiosity was not political or martial, but rather about the expected linguistic similarities.

IV. A Language Is a Nation

If this conflict had occurred a few centuries ago, such a question would have been unimaginable since the languages had not yet diverged from their common ancestor, the East Slavic language, which was spoken in both Russia and Ukraine in the form of dialects of the same language. Kurdish, lacking a unified formal standard, is today more akin to the historical stage and circumstances of East Slavic than to contemporary Russian or Ukrainian. Each of these two integrated languages is more similar to Kurmanji and Sorani than to a generic Kurdish. Historically, when the Russian and Ukrainian masses spoke the same language, they were considered a single nation. After the linguistic split, that is when dialects evolved into independent languages, the single nation split as well.

Consider a Kurd from Ilam (a Laki dialect speaker) traveling to Urmia (where Kurmanji is dominant). Would they be able to use Laki for smooth conversation in the market, or would Persian be more practical as a lingua franca? Similarly, in South Kurdistan, would a visitor from Khanaqin communicate smoothly with a salesman in the Zakho market without struggling with dialectal differences or switching to Arabic, the local lingua franca? The use of Persian, Arabic, and Turkish in Iran, Iraq, and Turkey for cross-dialectal communication is due to each language having a unified formal variety that bridges linguistic gaps across regions, a feature Kurdish lacks.

Reflecting on the Russia-Ukraine war and comparing the current state of Kurdish to the historical East Slavic, one might wonder: will Kurdish dialects such as Kurmanji, Sorani, Zaza, and Laki eventually become separate languages? Could future generations witness conflicts between two newly formed nations named Kurmanji and Sorani? The absence of a standardized common variety creates a vacuum among dialects, allowing them to develop distinct identities and potentially achieve the status of fully-fledged independent languages. Consequently, their speakers might come to see themselves as belonging to separate, newly-formed nations.

V. Language Ideology

"One does not inhabit a country; one inhabits a language."

E.M. Cioran

In sociolinguistics, the concept of ideology pertains to the adaptation, interaction, and common perception of a language from the viewpoint of its speaking communities. *Language ideology* lies at the core of the relationship and mutual influence between a nation and its language, forming the basis for language planning and policy.

It is defined as a set of beliefs about a language held by its speakers (Silverstein, 1979, p. 193, 248).

Judith Irvine (1989) defines it as:

"*the cultural system of ideas about social and linguistic relationships, together with their loading of moral and political interests.*"

An integrated language is an essential component of national identity; thus, lifestyle, religion, and social norms significantly influence linguistic affiliation and the degree of affinity between a society and its language. Common language ideology greatly enhances national sentiments, reinforcing ethnic belonging and promoting national solidarity.

For instance, Persian speakers often describe their language as "sweet as sugar" with the idiom "فارسی شکر است," reflecting a collective sense of the language's beauty. This widespread perception strengthens the language, supports its legitimacy, and underpins Iran's "*single language for the nation*" policy. Similarly, the Turkish, through a strong sense of self-image and veneration, has fostered increased nationalist sentiments and bolstered the success of Turkification efforts in Kurdistan. Arabic, is not only valued for its beauty and power, as the speakers claim, but also possesses a sacred status that encourages acquisition, practice, and scholarly research even by non-Arab Muslims.

In Western countries, despite individual linguistic freedoms, language policies significantly promote national languages. For example, the sustained support for English in America through robust tools that absorb social developments has garnered public backing for a similar to Iran's "*single language for the nation*" policy.

Conversely, when language prominence declines among its speakers and dialectal pride supersedes common linguistic standards, there is a subsequent decline in literary production, sociocultural cohesion, and political prosperity, ultimately weakening national solidarity even on major critical issues.

Neglecting the role of language ideology inflames dialectal competition and further augments the phenomenon of *dialectal purism*. Purism connotes praising the sense of regionality and the superiority of speakers of a certain dialect (variety) over others. The spread of purism in the Kurdish culture indicates the reason behind the prominence of regional-linguistic variations over the common (unified) standards. Purism is more noticeable among speakers of Kurdish than in other languages and it prioritizes dialectal affinity almost to the level of national sentiments, where dialect names often annex the national identity as evidenced by the frequent use of sub-national endonyms like Kurdish-Sorani, Kurdish-Faili, and Kurdish-Zaza.

The low prestige of Kurdish is evident in the tendency of its speakers to switch to other languages in multilingual conversations, rather than encouraging others to learn Kurdish. This behavior extends beyond business requirements and is notably prevalent in tourist areas, depriving visitors of the opportunity to explore the local culture. This indifference signifies low linguistic morale, a habit not observed among speakers of higher-prestige languages in the region.

With rapid global sociocultural changes and the emergence of multicultural societies around the world, and potentially in the Middle East, the Kurdish language faces significant challenges in maintaining its popularity among speakers. A well-supported language ideology, with affirmative policies and strategic planning, is essential for preserving Kurdish in its speaking community and ensuring its survival in the future competitive landscape.

5.1 Stratum (Language Prestige)

In multilingual regions, languages often vary in prestige and influence, a concept known as **Stratum**. The language with higher prestige, termed the *superstratum*, can influence and alter the language at a lower prestige level, known as the *substratum*.

The popularity of each variety in multilingual communities is valued based on cultural preferences reflecting diverse prestigious merits. For instance, urban culture often adds value to city dialects, where modern language patterns are more prevalent compared to rural. In Turkey, the state officially promotes Turkish in cities, aiming to monopolize the superstratum status and prevent the Kurdish language from developing prestigious sociolinguistic expressions. As a result, Turkish holds the highest stratum, making it the first choice in the region and leaving Kurdish in a subordinate position. The success of this policy is evident in the behavior of educated Kurdish speakers, who often borrow words related to urban life from the formal and academic Turkish language. The preference for loanwords over creating new Kurdish terms indicates a deficiency in the Kurdish lexicon, further relegating it to a substratum status. Consequently, as more borrowed words integrate into Kurdish, the stratum diminishes further. Similar dynamics are observed in Iran and Syria, where Persian and Arabic enjoy superior stratum and influence over Kurdish vocabulary since state policies in these countries have effectively lowered the linguistic prestige of Kurdish by hindering its lexical development.

5.1.1 Language Academy

Every language in the world undergoes linguistic transformations due to social changes and the expansion of human ideas. A language that fails to adapt to these developments gradually loses its prestige and rank of priority, becomes vulnerable, and may eventually face decomposition and extinction. Language academies are essential authorized bodies that aim to keep pace with linguistic updates, maintain the language's status, and ensure its functionality. These institutions are responsible for developing plans to enhance the orthographic structure, preserve the unity of formal dialects, and continuously serve as regulatory bodies, typically in a conservative manner.

Prominent linguists and literary figures, dedicated to elevating these languages to competitive status, are often permanently employed for this mission. They are tasked with studying, updating, and publishing official dictionaries, setting linguistic rules, and suggesting state language policies for implementation by the authorities. Examples of such academies include

- ✓ Académie Française *"The French Academy"*. Officially established in Paris, in 1635.

- ✓ האקדמיה ללשון העברית *"The Academy of the Hebrew Language"*. Formed as *The Hebrew Language Committee* in 1890 by the Russian linguist Eliezer Ben-Yehuda, and reestablished in Jerusalem in 1953.

- ✓ Türk Dil Kurumu *"The Turkish Language Association"*. Established in Ankara in 1932.

- ✓ فرهنگستان زبان وادب فارسی *"Academy of Persian Language and Literature"*, Established in Tehran in 1935 under the title فرهنگستان ایران *"Academy of Iran"*.

The first Kurdish cultural organization was founded in Baghdad in 1971, under the name *The Kurdish Culture Association* (جمعية الثقافة الكردية), as a result of the March Accord between the Iraqi government and the Kurdish revolutionary movement. The primary activities of this association included promoting Kurdish culture through

V. Language Ideology

publications such as the magazine "*Roji Kurdistan*" (رۆژی کوردستان) and its Arabic counterpart "شمس کردستان," as well as publishing Kurdish books. After enclosure, this establishment was reinitiated in Erbil in 2017 with the support of the Kurdish Regional Government, under the new name The Kurdish Academy (ئەکادیمیای کوردی).

The second official academy is the 'Kurdish Language Academy in Iran' فرهنگستان زبان کردی, founded in Tehran (2002) and recognized by the Iranian authority. (*)

Official recognition of such academies is crucial for implementing language policies, as it allows authorities to accept and support the proposed plans. However, linguistic research and suggested plans are not confined to official bodies; individual and group contributions also play a significant role in elevating the language's status and enhancing its ideology. On this account, the *Kurdish Academy of Language*, (†) despite lacking official support, was founded in London as a study center in 1992 by dedicated volunteers.

Despite the availability of numerous resources in recent years, substantial progress in Kurdish linguistic modification has been limited. For successful reform, an active official Kurdish linguistic body is required to draw plans for an ambitious future, to prepare a comprehensive corpus plan that builds on the foundational work of T. Wahbi and C. Bedirxan from the early 20th century.

A practical plan should recognize past achievements, identify and avoid previous mistakes, and provide guidance for observing and modifying the linguistic structure. A plan that reforms the spelling system, with promising official support is essential not only for creating a unified formal dialect but also for enhancing the language's prestige (stratum) and ensuring the first option is placed in the cross-dialectal conversation whenever mutual intelligibility comes short.

---

* https://akademiyakurdi.org
† https://kurdishacademy.org

5.2 Language Planning

Language planning is a regulatory activity aimed at managing and enhancing the function, structure, and deployment of a language through systematic observation and suggested changes to be implemented by the state.

Corpus planning, CP, may involve amending grammatical rules or updating the spelling system. Additionally, *status planning*, SP, may include proposals to improve the language's status and strategies to facilitate its deployment and dominance. For instance, an SP might recommend consolidating several minor linguistic varieties into a single dominant language to serve political or economic purposes. Conversely, a plan could advocate for a pluralistic policy that preserves the linguistic rights of minority groups.

Furthermore, *acquisition planning* (AP), facilitates and promotes the learning and use of a particular language for greater proficiency and widespread use among the population. AP ensures that the target language is effectively taught and learned.

In executing the endorsed language plan, authorities aim to ensure that the language remains functional and relevant in various domains, including education, government, and media.

5.2.1 Corpus Planning

The linguistic aspect of language development encompasses phonology, morphology, lexicographical structure, and grammatical rules.

Sociolinguist Robert L. Cooper (1989, p. 30) defines corpus planning as:

> *"the activity of preparing a normative orthography, grammar, and dictionary for the guidance of writers and speakers in a non-homogeneous speech community."*

V. Language Ideology

In line with this definition, addressing the current state of Kurdish language development necessitates planning that could achieve the following:

- ✓ **Facilitate the use of a unified grammar and select a single writing system**: Reform efforts should aim to streamline grammatical rules and orthographic conventions to ensure the required level of consistency across all dialects.

- ✓ **Revive the correct roots of morphemes from the common variety**: Considering the historical shifts in morphemes, drawing from the rich resources of Pahlavi roots may help in retrieving suitable affixes, thereby expanding the language's capacity to generate new phrases.

- ✓ **Purify and reduce borrowed words**: Efforts should focus on minimizing the use of loanwords that disrupt linguistic harmony and lower the language's prestige, particularly those introduced through Arabization and Turkification.

- ✓ **Approximate standards for grammar, writing system, and lexicon**: These standards should be adjusted to a level of intelligibility that is accessible to most if not all, speakers of Kurdish varieties.

- ✓ **Create professional vocabularies**: Developing specialized terms for fields such as legislation, politics, and sports is crucial for the language's modern functionality.

- ✓ **Enhance mutual intelligibility among Kurdish-speaking communities**: Prioritizing shared vocabulary across dialects and reducing dialect-specific cognates can improve communication and cohesion among different Kurdish-speaking groups.

These measures are intended to strengthen the language, ensuring its relevance and functionality in various sociocultural and professional domains.

5.2.2 Status Planning

In linguistics, status planning (SP) is a type of linguistic effort that focuses on the societal role and function of a language within a given community or country. It involves plans to influence and change the societal uses and recognition of a language, often aiming to enhance its prestige, expand its domains of use, or establish it as an official language. It can also involve efforts to support (or repress) minority languages and ensure their continued use in specific contexts.

Kurdish, in general, imperatively requires a conscious SP to address the current linguistic ambiguities, such as the unclear distinction between what necessarily constitutes a language versus the flexibility of a dialect, the priority for official or colloquial use in various domains, and the level of standardization. An SP also determines whether to value colloquial diversity as a source of linguistic richness or to view it as an obstacle to linguistic and national unity. In the absence of a unified formal Kurdish, unplanned circumstances have granted official status to Sorani and Kurmanji. Without a status plan, other dialects may gain the same status, preventing the emergence of a unifying variety.

In addition to transitioning Kurdish from a collection of dialects to an integrated and modified form, status planning also involves purification efforts. Kurdification aims to replace the dominance of Arabic and Turkish with a Kurdish lexicon while, at the same time, considering morphological roots and maintaining a practical degree of kinship with Persian and other Iranic-based varieties.

Unlike corpus planning, which requires scholars and experts to develop a plan through academic procedures, status planning needs an authoritative body for meticulous execution. Although a status plan may seem unrealistic and less capable of competing with the well-established, government-backed plans of Ankara and Tehran regarding Kurdish, having an existing scheme ready will facilitate the unification of the formal variety and the transition from Turkish and Persian to a unified Kurdish language when the opportunity arises.

5.2.3 Acquisition Planning

Acquisition planning (AP) is a field dedicated to the strategies and mechanisms required to enhance the acquisition of a language by its speakers and facilitate learning for non-speakers. As a form of language management, AP aims to enhance language teaching, distribute literature, and encourage social groups to develop interest and proficiency in the language (Spolsky, 2004, p. 8). It involves promoting the official variety in educational settings, media, and literary uses as an alternative to colloquial forms. The plan employs various methods to increase language visibility and acceptance. These methods include deploying the language prominently in public signage, such as traffic signs, shopfronts, and restaurant menus, as well as in the public names of streets, schools, and hospitals. The state also reinforces language presence through the spelling of towns and suburbs, and by leveraging mass media and the arts to link the language with national identity. Furthermore, AP emphasizes involving the public in discussions and keeping the speaker population informed about future applications and transitional stages. Public seminars and extensive explanations of the project's motives, necessity, and goals help attract broader publicity and improve public engagement, particularly when applying new corpus plans. In general, AP is not only essential for effective language learning but also plays a crucial role in preserving and revitalizing endangered or minority languages; facilitates access to education, employment, and social services; helps foster a sense of national unity and cultural identity; bridges linguistic divides, promoting mutual understanding and social cohesion; and in an increasingly globalized world, enhances a nation's global competitiveness.

For Kurdish, recent usage trends indicate the necessity for an active and authoritative language academy. The body can develop comprehensive plans for covering the process of corpus status, and acquisition planning.

In general, CP establishes the foundation of linguistic unity, SP enhances the language's prestige, and AP in turn facilitates learning, connects Kurdish with the collective consciousness of its speakers, and mitigates the influence of other (official) languages in predominantly Kurdish-speaking areas.

5.3 Language Policy

The term **language policy** refers to the set of principles and decisions implemented by governmental or authoritative bodies to regulate and influence the use, structure, and function of languages within a given community or country. It encompasses various aspects, including planning, rights, and the promotion or suppression of specific languages or dialects.

It is defined by UNESCO as:

"Official government decisions regarding the use of language in the public domain, including courts, schools, government offices and health services." (*)

A policy is more of a political set of legislation than linguistic, usually suggested by an official language regulator body. Robert B. Kaplan and Richard B. Baldauf (1997, p. xi) provide the following sociolinguistic definition:

"A body of ideas, laws, regulations, rules and practices intended to achieve the planned language change in the societies, group or system."

States often seek to promote or limit the use of certain language varieties over others, motivated by economic considerations to enhance communication or driven by nationalistic or racially discriminatory ideologies.

While some states globally design policies to protect and promote regional and ethnic languages at risk of extinction, the majority of Middle Eastern countries adhere to strict monolingual policies. These policies enforce the exclusive use of one language in official and sometimes even oral communication, thereby suppressing others. This approach is particularly prevalent among the three major languages in the region: Turkish, Arabic, and Persian. The vast majority of Middle Eastern systems adopt the policy of *a single*

---

* EFA global monitoring report; Education for all: literacy for life, UNESCO report 2006; p 420

V. Language Ideology

language for a single nation, with no recognition of minority languages or use in administrative or influential fields such as education, legislation, or the judiciary.

5.3.1 Turkish Policy

In Turkey, the language policy has pursued a rigorous Turkification strategy since the late Ottoman Empire, aimed at transforming the country from a multilingual to a homogenous Turkish state. In 1913, the government established a paramilitary training program for young ultra-nationalists, known as the *Association of Turkish Strength Promotion*. This initiative aimed to enforce Turkish as the sole language within the empire's borders, where the defense ministry provided volunteers with free rifles (Akmeşe, 2005).

Following the collapse of the Ottoman Empire and the rise of extreme nationalism, the Republic of Turkey intensified its Turkification efforts under Ataturk's leadership. Legislative measures divided non-Turkish-speaking regions into four zones based on the percentage of Turkish speakers, regulating Turkification through population displacement (Bedirxan, 1934):

- ✓ Zone 1: Areas requiring an increase in Turkish speakers.

- ✓ Zone 2: Regions accommodating non-Turkish speakers who should be integrated into Turkish culture.

- ✓ Zone 3: Lands where immigrants with Turkish culture could reside freely without assistance.

- ✓ Zone 4: Non-Turkish-speaking regions from which the population should be evacuated.

The primary goal of Turkification has been to eliminate the existence of other local languages, particularly Kurdish, not only within the Turkish Republic's borders but also in neighboring countries. For instance, Turkey significantly contributed to the abolition of the Kurdish Soviet Republic of Kurduyezd, colloquially known as Red Kurdistan, during Stalin's rule in 1929, displacing its population in distant Soviet regions like Kazakhstan and Siberia. In recent decades, despite the substantial progress in Turkification and the resulting decline in the indigenous languages of Kurdistan, the state has permitted limited television and radio broadcasts in Kurdish, under the pressure of satellite channels broadcasting from Western Europe and the Iraqi-Kurdistan region. However, Kurdish and other native languages remain prohibited in administrative, educational, and judicial sectors.

At the time the official linguistic policy aims to normalize Turkish dialects by promoting a single prestigious variety with a superstratum status and approximating the entire Turanian language family, there are attempts to accentuate the differences between Kurdish dialects, particularly Zaza and Kurmanji, to hinder Kurdish linguistic unity. Additionally, Turkish state broadcaster TRT limits most Kurdish-language broadcasts to rural affairs, thereby associating Turkish with modern urban life, away from the modern lifestyle.

5.3.2 Syrian Policy

Arabic is established as the sole official language of Syria. This status is enshrined in the country's constitution and reinforced through various laws and policies. Practically it is the sole language of government, education, and the judiciary.

Since gaining independence, the ultra-nationalist Syrian regimes have enforced a strict language policy to establish the dominance of Arabic over other languages within the state. The only period during which Kurdish publications were permitted was under the French Mandate (1922–1943). The most notable publication of that period was the magazine "Hawar" (The Salvation Cry), founded by the pioneering linguist Celadet Bedirxan (Jaladat Badrakhan). Hawar released its first issue on May 15, 1932, and continued until its final issue on August 16, 1943, producing a total of 57 issues.

After Syria's independence, the new Arab Republic authorities seized the magazine as part of their new linguistic policy. Since independence, authorities, driven by an extreme nationalist doctrine, have imposed stringent measures against the use of minority languages. Kurdish and others were prohibited in the media,

V. Language Ideology

education, and judiciary fields. However, despite this historical setback, Hawar introduced the orthography that was later adopted to become the modern writing system for Kurmanji.

Currently, the very first sentence in the Constitution of 2012 commenced with the word 'Arab' followed by the second paragraph:

"The Syrian Arab Republic is proud of its Arab identity and the fact that its people are an integral part of the Arab nation."

Denying the existence of national minorities is reinforced in Article 1:

"The people of Syria are part of the Arab nation"

In addition, the Constitution did not mention in its text any language other than Arabic, Article 4 stipulates:

"The official language of the state is Arabic."

However, after the liberation of the majority of Kurdish speaking landscape, this restrictive language policy has persisted only in areas controlled by the Syrian government, in contrast, the autonomous Kurdish-controlled region, *North and Northeastern Syria*, has allowed the use of minority languages within its administrative borders, granting rights that are denied by the central government.

5.3.3 Iraqi Policy

As part of cultural traits, Arabic, in general, encourages linguistic purification, replacing borrowed words with coined native equivalents and Arabizing worldwide common phrases and terms, thereby maintaining linguistic purity. This process of nativization covers all vocabulary areas; including scientific, political, and sports terminology, and names of products and places.

Nonetheless, Iraqi authorities have adopted a relatively inclusive policy towards minorities, enacting the first constitution in the Middle East that allows for the use of two official languages. Kurdish is explicitly recognized as the second official and serves as the administrative language in the Kurdistan region, with no restrictions in education, media, or the judiciary. This openness towards minority cultures, stemming from the Kurdish national struggle, has extended to other languages, particularly in the Kurdistan region, where speakers of Turkmen and Assyrian languages significantly benefit from the atmosphere of tolerance. The Iraqi Constitution of 2005 recognizes Arabic and Kurdish as the official languages of the country (Article 4). This constitutional guarantee ensures the use of both languages in governmental, administrative, educational, and legal contexts within the Kurdistan region and to some extent across Iraq.

Mentioned that, in the Arab regions of the country (Middle and Southern Iraq), the authorities still neglect the linguistic rights of the minorities, such as the use of public education or media broadcasting in local languages including Kurdish for Kurds residing in these regions.

5.3.4 Iranian Policy

The first constitution of modern Iran, enacted in 1906, did not explicitly designate an official language, nor did the amendment of 1946. This absence implicitly allowed local municipalities to exercise linguistic liberties based on locally used varieties. The first legal reference to an official language was included in the *Constitution of the Islamic Republic of Iran*, 1979, which mandated that official communication be conducted in Persian. However, it also permitted the use of local and ethnic languages in publications and media, and allowed for the teaching of local literature in schools alongside Persian:

> *"The official language and writing script is Persian, however, regional and ethnic languages are allowed in the press and mass media, as well as for teaching of their literature in schools besides Persian."* (*)

---

* Constitution of the Islamic Republic of Iran, Chapter 2, Article 15.

"اسناد و مکاتبات م متون رسمی و کتب رسمی باید با زبان و خط فارسی باشد، ولی استفاده از زبان های محلی و قومی در مطبوعات و رسانه های گروهی و تدریس ادبیات آنها در مدارس، در کنار زبان فارسی، آزاد است"

V. Language Ideology

According to Article 15 (Chapter II), the 75 minority languages, which are the mother tongues of 39% of the population, (*) are officially allowed to teach their own literature. Nevertheless, ambiguity persists in distinguishing between *"teaching the language"* and *"teaching literature beside Persian"*. This issue is raised by Dr. Muhammad Riza Hay'at, an Azeri-speaking scholar:

> *"(teaching literature) of (local and ethnic languages) is allowed, not teaching their language and literature. Undoubtedly, the framers of this Article [15] were able to recognize the difference between language and literature, but for reasons that are obvious to almost everyone, they deliberately opposed the teaching of language. (Literature teaching) means that Turkish, Kurdish, Arab, Baloch, Turkmen, etc. poets and writers should be introduced in Persian, this will not only not help non-Persian languages in Iran, but will also increase the influence of Persian on the literature of other languages."* (†)

Besides Persian, Arabic is recognized as the language of religion and is regulated within the Iranian national curriculum. Constitution stipulates:

> *"Since Arabic is the language of the Qur'an and Islamic sciences and knowledge and Persian literature is completely mixed with it, this language should be taught in all classes and disciplines after elementary until the end of secondary school."* (‡)

---

* https://minorityrights.org/country/iran
† https://tebarens.com/fa/مسئله-زبان-و-ضرورت-تغییر-قانون-اساسی-دک

Continued from previous page:

"در ادامه این اصل تنها تدریس ادبیات زبان‌های محلی و قومی مجاز شمرده شده است نه تدریس زبان و ادبیات آن‌ها. بدون شک تنظیم کنندگان این اصل، قادر به تشخیص تفاوت زبان و ادبیات بوده‌اند، اما بنا به دلایلی که تقریباً بر همه واضح است، عمداً با تدریس زبان مخالفت کرده‌اند. "تدریس ادبیات" بدین معنی است که شعرا و نویسندگان ترک و کرد و عرب و بلوچ و ترکمن و ... باید به زبان فارسی معرفی شوند. و این نه تنها هیچ کمکی به زبان‌های غیر فارسی در ایران نخواهد کرد، بلکه تأثیر و نفوذ زبان فارسی بر ادبیات سایر زبان‌ها را نیز افزایش خواهد داد."

‡ Constitution of the Islamic Republic of Iran, Chapter 2, Article 15.

Historically, Iranian policy has not restricted the use of major linguistic varieties in the press and mass media. The country has embraced multilingualism in radio and television since its inception, accommodating various vernacular varieties. After the establishment of the first radio station, "Radio Tehran," in 1940, Azari language programs commenced in Tabriz, the major Azari-speaking city, with the launch of "Radio Tabriz" in 1946. This step was followed by Kurdish broadcasting through "Radio Kermanshah" in 1959 (*). Currently, over 30 provincial TV channels offer programs in local languages, supplemented by multilingual satellite broadcasting by numerous corporations, including the state-run Islamic Republic of Iran Broadcasting.

The Islamic Revolution, however, has prioritized ideological concerns over linguistic ones. The efforts to promote Persian as the sole official language are not rooted in nationalist fanaticism but are aimed at maintaining a unified ideological stance and reinforcing the central power's cohesion. This political agenda is evident in the limited support for linguistic institutions, such as the Academy of Persian Language and Literature, and the passive stance towards loanwords, with no significant efforts to nativize cognates or reduce the borrowed vocabulary. Foreign words in Persian constitute about 40% of lexical items (Owens, 2013, p. 352).

An example of ideological (religious) priorities superseding linguistic unity is Iran's rejection of a proposal to establish a joint television network with other Persian-speaking countries, suggested by Tajikistan and welcomed by Afghanistan in 2011. After five years of consideration, Iran declined the project due to ideological (sectarian) differences with these countries, demonstrating the preference for maintaining religious doctrine over linguistic cooperation. (†)

---

* https://www.irannamag.com/en/article/advent-development-radio-iran/
† https://farsnews.ir/news/9003022712%20%20%20%20/-مشترك-تلویزیون هاي-C8%80%2E%-زبان-و-چالشC8%80%2E%کشورهاي-فارسي-رو-2C8%80%2E%پیش

V. Language Ideology

5.3.5 Kurdish Policy

Despite its official status in Iraq, where it is formally the primary language in territories administered by the Kurdistan Regional Government (KRG) and de facto in northern Syria, Kurdish has not yet achieved the level of prestige necessary to firmly establish itself as a distinct means of communication throughout the Kurdish-speaking homeland. The primary reason for this low status is that Kurdish has been systematically marginalized by stringent language policies enforced in Turkey, Iran, and Syria. Even with official recognition in Iraq, Kurdish continues to struggle under the dominance of widely used Arabic. Nonetheless, there has been no significant effort to enhance the role of Kurdish to align with modern lifestyles or to establish a unified standard that reflects national unity. The lack of a clear policy has perpetuated the stereotype of Kurdish as a collection of sectarian dialects rather than a mature, integral language.

Given the increasing pace of global cultural integration, the emergence of multicultural communities, and the inter-linguistic environment, it is imperative to follow and implement a well-structured linguistic policy. Additionally, assimilation measures in Kurdish-speaking regions necessitate a vigilant Kurdish policy to counteract efforts by neighboring countries to undermine the language's status. The goal of a Kurdish language policy, if adopted by the KRG or the Rojava administration, is to enable it to combat decline, maintain integrity, and keep pace with social developments.

A comprehensive Kurdish language policy should aim to achieve the following objectives:

- ✓ **Creating a Unified Classical Dialect**: To develop a unified classical dialect supported by status and acquisition plans to gain acceptance among the entire speaking population. Promote this unified dialect as the primary linguistic reference for Kurdish in international institutions and media centers.

- ✓ **Enhancing Dialectal Intelligibility**: To utilize media, drama, and visual arts to improve mutual understanding among different Kurdish dialects.

- ✓ **Overcoming Purist Tendencies**: To address the negative purist tendency that assigns varying degrees of "Kurdishness" to different dialects. The policy improves social coherence by fostering inclusivity.

- ✓ **Elevating Kurdish Status**: To shift the status of Kurdish to a superstratum level within Kurdish-speaking regions in relation to other languages.

- ✓ **Counteracting Adverse Policies**: To oppose detrimental policies, such as Turkey's efforts to create a divide between Kurmanji and Zaza, and similar policies in Iran and Iraq that depict Pahlawani (Faili) as diluted and less pure on the scale of "Kurdishness."

A well-planned Kurdish language policy is essential for preserving the language's integrity and promoting its development in the face of external challenges and internal diversity.

VI. Phonology & Orthography

"To imagine a language is to imagine a form of life"

Ludwig Wittgenstein

A language is not just a dictionary, since it is not only a list of words; a language is more a relation of words than a word collection. That is, the sense lies in the sentence, which follows grammatical and syntactical rules to produce meaning. A speaker of Arabic, for instance, can understand the majority of the Maltese vocabulary and half of Persian, but cannot engage himself in a Maltese or Persian conversation. Regardless of oral factors such as phonology, pitch, intonation, and prosody that affect the level of understanding, syntax, grammar, and language patterns are more effective for mutual understanding.

In theory, a word by itself has no intrinsic value; it is just an abstract concept, a sign with no informational worth. For instance, the word 'car' by itself does not inform on its color, size, model, owner, when was it, where, etc. The value of a word evolves only by its sequence in a group of words, i.e., when it exists in a sentence. According to F. De Saussure, a word has a sound image a *'signifier'*, and a conceptual meaning a *'signified'*. The signifier has no intrinsicality, and the signified does not hold a true value.

To exemplify, the phonemes or letters of the word 'tree', as a signifier, have no sense of association with what it represents; different languages may use different phonemes and letters to represent the same signified concept (the concept of the tree). Words like 'дерево' /ˈdʲerʲɪvə/, 'درخت' /dɪrˈext/, or 'dar' /dˈɑːr/ (cognates in Russian, Persian, and Kurdish) can equally signify the same signified (the essence of a tree).

Also, the signified by itself is an abstract entity (virtual) and only becomes informative when it is accompanied by details in the correct syntactical order.

"Signs function, then, not through their intrinsic value but through their relative position." (De Saussure, 1959, p. 118)

Since a word per se has no value, the sense is determined only by the word position within a sentence—that is, the word cannot form sense without a syntax rule (the order that determines which word denotes the subject and which one represents the object). Syntax order, in turn, is part of the wider domain of rules that encompasses conjugation and semantics. This structure is universal across all languages, yet what is language-specific is the syntactical order of words, the grammar system, the lexicon, as well as phonological specificity—these are the building blocks of every language.

In addition to the phonetic representation, orthography (the writing system) is a symbolic portrayal of the words. Both phonological and orthographic signifiers are correlated ways of expression. However, due to the widespread publications covering vital aspects of modern life such as scientific, legislative, and political documentation, the role of orthography is rising while the sound structure is retreating from its all-time hegemony. Therefore, language is no longer a mere vocal gesture, but in one of its aspects has become a scriptural instrument of communication, and just as the language needs to review phonetic shifts, it has become equally necessary to develop and maintain the orthographic besides phonological representation of senses.

6.1 Phonetics & Phonology

When hearing the word "language," the first impression that pops into the mind is not its writing system but rather the speech sounds (the ton and intonation). Languages such as Italian, French, and Arabic are easily distinguishable by certain phonemes and intonation without prerequisites to understanding the meanings. There are two

VI. Phonology & Orthography

fields of linguistics concerned with sounds: *phonetics*, which deals with the production of human sounds in the vocal tract, and *phonology*, which considers the relationship between sounds and meanings.

Phonetics is the science that studies sound generation, regardless of any specific language, while phonology is language-specific, concerned with the sound patterns and how they convey meanings.

Together, phonetics and phonology offer a comprehensive understanding of how humans produce, perceive, and use sounds in communication.

6.1.1 Phonetics

Phonetics is a branch of linguistics that focuses on the classification and production of speech sounds in terms of the articulatory mechanisms of the human vocal tract, what sounds are, and how they are perceived by listeners. (Yule, 1985, p.26,41) The three branches of phonetics science are:

Articulatory: the study of how speech sounds are made or articulated, like the positioning of the vocal organs to allow different paths for the air in order to produce different sounds. The articulation involves the coordinated movement of the lips, tongue, teeth, palate, and respiratory system; it often determines the sound of the word.

Auditory: the study of the listener's perception of sounds via the ear. It is concerned with hearing and understanding—that is, the meaning of the speech from the listener's perspective, not the speaker's.

Acoustic: studies the physical properties of speech as sound waves in the air that are determined by measuring pitch (formants and frequencies), loudness, and quality.

6.1.2 Phonology

Unlike phonetics, the science that is concerned with sound production regardless of which language is in use, phonology deals with sound structure in individual languages—that is, how a certain language uses sound patterns to create meaning. George Yule defines phonology (1985, p. 42) as:

"the description of the systems and patterns of speech sounds in a language ... concerned with the abstract or mental aspect of the sounds in language rather than with the actual physical articulation of speech sounds".

As a theoretical concept, a phoneme in phonology represents a combination of different articulation sounds that are similar to some degree and are usually associated with (represented by) one grapheme (letter) in the writing system. Nonetheless, a phoneme ignores, at the same time, the minor phonetic differences. For instance, while the phonetics distinguish the light allophone 'L' /l/ from the dark /ɫ/, as they are produced by different articulations, phonology may neglect the difference, considering both as two allophones of the same phoneme. English phonology assigns a single grapheme 'L' for both, as in 'Ball' /bɔɫ/ and 'Law' /lɔ/. Persian and Arabic writing systems follow the same phonological rule. The dark allophone appears in words like 'Allah' الله /æɫˈɫɑːh/ (Eng. God), while light /l/ occurs in 'Elah' إله /ɪlˈɑːh/ (Eng. Divine), however, these languages use a single grapheme 'ل' for both sounds. In contrast, the Russian writing system considers these shades as two different phonemes by representing the light phoneme /l/ with the grapheme 'л' alone, as in the word 'Nedeale' неделя /nɪːdɪeleɪˈ/ (Eng. Week), while trailing it with 'ы' for dark allophone, as in the word 'Bealy' Белый /bɪəɫjːˈ/ (Eng. White).

Kurdish, however, represents the phoneme inconsistently, while the Kurmanji writing system neglects the difference. Sorani distinguishes the light from the dark by the diacritic 'ˇ' over the letter 'ل' as in 'lau' /laːʊˈ/ لاو (Eng. Youth) and 'Balam' /beɫɑːmˈ/ بەڵام (Eng. But).

A consonant phoneme is usually a spectrum of different shades, like 'V' as in 'Victor' and 'Voice', 'B' as in 'Basket' and 'Butter', and 'M' as in 'Mint' and 'Mother'. Most languages, like English, ignore multiple

VI. Phonology & Orthography

shades that constitute a single phoneme; however, some others exceptionally distinguish the shades. The Polish language refers to the sound 'Sh' /ʃ/ with two shades represented by 'Ś' as in 'Miś' (Eng. Teddy Bear) and 'Sz' as in 'Szyja' (Eng. Neck); Sorani Kurdish differentiates the light and dark 'R' as in the first 'ڕ' and second occurrence 'ر' of the sound 'R' in 'Robar' ڕووبار (English River).

6.1.3 Phonetic Bias

Oral/aural exchange of phonetically produced symbols is always affected by changes in individual and communal articulating habits and auditory aptitudes. Thus, by transferring linguistic patterns from one generation to the other, this individual-specific pronunciation and auditory perception cause a constant phonetic bias over time. As a result, allophones are gradually shifted through generations, resulting in the replacement of existing phonemes and phonetic features. This phonetic bias is the reason why isolated communities develop their own speech patterns, composing distinct vocabulary that differs from the others, by which the individuals find a way of communicating with the members of the same community easier than with other populations.

Long isolation or even weak connections among groups create distinct accents and evolve dialects; hence, after longer periods, when reaching the point of losing mutual intelligibility, group dialects turn into separate languages. Within this path of evolution, Kurdish varieties evolved from the early form of Kurdish (that is, before the current dialect came into existence), which, in turn, branched earlier from West-Iranic and, itself, branched earlier from Proto-Iranic. Linguistic genealogy can trace the roots of Kurdish back to Proto-Indo-European, the language that (theoretically) existed during the Late Neolithic to Early Bronze Age, approximately from 4500 to 2500 BCE. (Gimbutas, 1974) The phonetic biases, besides other factors that led to the birth of Kurdish as a separate language, naturally led to the emergence, in a later stage, of differences between the currently prevailing dialects of Kurmanji, Sorani, Pahlawani, and Zaza/Gorani. These dialects are anticipated to develop further into independent languages within the forthcoming centuries. On the other hand, the contemporary lifestyle, with the luxury of easy transportation, widespread media channels, and the persistence of orthographic systems, affords the ability to preserve the current form of languages for longer or even approximate these varieties to raise mutual intelligibility.

Phonetic bais is a prominent factor in evolving accents, dialects, ethnolects, and languages; thus, it is a constant threat to linguistic unity. However, carefully crafted and unified phonological standards may absorb phonetic shifts and preserve the continuity of the language in the same form for longer.

6.2 Writing systems

Using combined symbols as a visual representation of thoughts can be traced back to cave drawings made at least 20,000 years ago. However, the earliest writing for which we have clear evidence, the "cuneiform" marked on clay tablets in Sumer, and the hieroglyphics in Egypt, a few centuries later, go back only about 5,000 years. Having said that, for simplicity, the logo-syllabic scripting (logo for morpheme i.e. a symbol for word) was replaced by the Phoenician script (grapheme for phoneme – that is a letter for basic sound). That is, the writing systems in use today can be identified in inscriptions dated only around 3,000 years ago. (Yule, 1958, p212) Hence, modern writing systems are standardized by orthographic rules for better comprehension, enhancing fluency, and maintaining the unity of the lexicon. Orthography is defined by the Oxford Dictionary as:

> "The formal term for spelling or for the subject of spelling as a linguistic study" (*)

---

* Oxford Reference
https://www.oxfordreference.com/display/10.1093/oi/authority.20110803100255163

VI. Phonology & Orthography

Conventional spelling and punctuation are critical for a clear representation of ideas; without them, transmitting scientific theories is cumbersome and fallible. These conventions help make the texts of laws and legislation clearer, and the language becomes unsusceptible. Orthography preserves the lexical form of the word, even if the sound has been biased over the years. The lack of a distinct orthographic system is one of the reasons behind the abundance of Kurdish varieties and the low level of cross-dialectal intelligibility. If such a system existed, it would have agglutinated these varieties with a common linguistic form and attitude. In other words, if Kurdish and other Iranic-origin languages had continued using the Pahlavi writing system in a similar manner that Armenian, Arabic, Hebrew, and Georgian maintained theirs, the Pahlavi would have preserved a great deal of its integrity and, moreover, may have kept its ancient unity in the present time. In addition, a well-designed modified orthography would have leveled dialects.

6.2.1 Punctuation

Orthography is not only limited to letters and spellings; it is also concerned with punctuation marks; rules of punctuation are part of the convention and necessary to form the meaning of the sentence. Take this example:

A father called his children to gather for a meal (serving lunch). He shouted:

"We need to eat kids."

This sentence, if only read on paper, misleads the reader into a different meaning, depicting a group of cannibals about to eat children. But the meaning differs when the writer adds the punctuation mark (a comma) after the word 'eat'

"We need to eat, kids."

Some languages rely on punctuation more than others. In the Russian language, for instance, an interrogative sentence does not always begin with a corresponding adverb; it may follow the syntax of a declarative sentence, so it relies only on the question mark to distinguish between the two forms.

The sentence: "You cook well" is written as follows:

ты хорошо готовишь.

The interrogative sentence "Do you cook well?" also follows the same syntax, but it is only distracted by a question mark:

ты хорошо готовишь?

6.2.2 Lexical Stability

It is common to notice the inconsistency between spelling and pronunciation in many modern Western languages. This variability suggests that vocabulary updated the sound of the words over the past centuries while keeping the orthographical origin intact.

Taking English as an example, despite the diverted spelling in the American dialect, the language appears to be more phonetically vibrant while orthographically being conservative. It is a luxurious freedom in the West to utter the pronunciation for the comfort of the speaker rather than preserving the historical sound of the word. Unlike the Western languages, the speakers of the Aramaic-based orthography, tend to twist the comfortable vernacular phonetics to meet the traditionally agreed standards.

The reason why we do not perspicuously sense such a wide gap between spelling and sounds in Arabic and Persian is that the former inherited orthographic characteristics from Aramaic and the latter from Pahlavi, where both languages used writing systems that minimized the presence of vowel letters, replacing short vowels with diacritics. Moreover, modern writing omits these diacritics and entirely disregards short vowels such as /ʊ/ (as in 'Book'), /ʌ/ (as in 'Cut'), /ɪ/ (as in 'Sit'), and /e/ (as in 'Say'). The neglect of diacritics allows it to comprise all shades of short vowels within a single spelling. Western orthographies reflect precise pronunciation, making phonetic bias evident. Unlike Western systems, Arabic and

VI. Phonology & Orthography

Persian allow the spelling of a word to represent a wider range of pronunciations.

The technique of omitting short vowels was also adopted by Eliezer Ben-Yehuda in his project that marked the miracle revival of Hebrew in 1881.

One may notice that despite assigning graphemes for short vowels, as part of the Kurdish (both writing systems) and Turkish spellings, there is still a harmony between spelling and habitual pronunciation, this is mainly due to the fact that these writing systems are relatively new (no more than a century old); as such, phonetic bias has not yet gone long enough to create a noticeable disharmony.

However, the consistency between spelling and pronunciation in both Kurdish systems, as well as Turkish, may not last for long. It is possible for inconsistency to emerge from future phonetic updates, urging for a new set of orthographic reforms in the forthcoming centuries. On the other hand, Arabic, Hebrew, and Persian will be more resilient and capable of absorbing the phonetic bias.

6.2.3 Rephonemicization

As the vocal tract is unique to individuals and phonemes are getting rearranged over time, some old ones may disappear or be replaced by newly emerged phonemes. A language's phonological structure may well be affected by this natural process, and the language may sound different over different courses of time. The continuous sound change is called rephonemicization. In order to maintain phonological structure, authorized linguists, as part of corpus planning, periodically react to this phenomenon in one of the following procedures, liberal, conservative, or restricted approaches:

a. **Liberal approach:** Updating the language's orthography elements to suit modern usages similar to Hebrew and Chinese.

b. **Conservative approach**: Maintaining the old spelling while allowing shifted pronunciation, such as in English and French.

c. **Restricted approach:** Compromise the vernacular phonetics to adopt the traditions, such as Arabic.

6.2.3.1 Liberal Approach

In response to rephonemicization, a linguistic body may develop a comprehensive corpus plan for significant modifications to the orthographic system. A notable example is the Russian language reform following the October Revolution. On the first day of 1918, the Bolshevik authorities mandated a transition from the traditional orthographic system to a new one based on Dr. Alexei Shakhmatov's simplification proposal. Similarly, in 1958, China implemented a major reform that simplified over 36% of frequently used characters and limited their usage to only 6,196 characters.

6.2.3.2 Conservative Approach

Minor updates may suffice to normalize linguistic patterns. While preserving the existing system, the creation of new graphemes or the modification of certain word spellings could address the need for reform. Numerous instances illustrate a conservative approach to linguistic modification. For example, American English underwent significant changes following the reforms initiated by Noah Webster in his 1806 publication, *A Compendious Dictionary of the English Language*. Similarly, the Académie Française recommended spelling changes in 1990 that impacted over 2,000 French words. A comparable approach was adopted for the German language reform in 1996.

6.2.3.3 Restricted Approach

Liturgical languages such as Arabic are resistant to modification due to the sanctity of scripts. Thus, there is always a persistent tendency to adjust vernacular pronunciations to align with the original and historic sounds of words, including unused phonemes, rather than altering the orthographic structure. However, modern standards in publications have introduced a noticeable change by omitting diacritics. These diacritics, known as Harkat (حركات), represent short vowels: /ʊ/ ὄ, /ɪ/ ọ, /e/ ó, /ʊn/ ȍ, /ɪn/ ọ, /en/ ó, the sign of stress (ȍ), and the silence (ȍ). Despite their omission in

VI. Phonology & Orthography

modern publications, diacritics and short vowels remain integral to the grammar.

Similarly, modern Hebrew omits its diacritics, Niqqud (נִקֻּד), which also represent short vowels. These are now only used when there is a need to reveal the correct sound of a word, primarily with unconventional and foreign words, and in teaching children proper pronunciation.

In conclusion, the representation of short vowels by diacritics rather than letters, and their omission in modern publications allows for a broader range of pronunciations and the integration of various accents and dialects within a single spelling. This approach is ideal for a reformed Kurdish orthography.

6.2.4 Orthographic Depth

When orthography allows a high degree of precision in the correspondence between graphemes (letters) and phonemes (sounds)—meaning the spelling is consistent with the sequence of sounds—the language is classified as transparent or orthographically shallow, and is referred to as a **phonemic** language.

Examples of such languages include Spanish and Italian in Europe and Turkish and Hindi in Asia. Conversely, when the graphemes do not correspond to the phonemes—meaning the sound differs from the spelling—the language is classified as opaque or deep, and is referred to as **nonphonemic**. Examples of opaque languages include English and French. However, the existence of fully ideal transparency in any language is disputed.

The degree of orthographic depth ranges from the most transparent, with a one-to-one correspondence between sounds and letters—such as Esperanto and Serbo-Croatian—to highly opaque languages like Chinese and French. Intermediate languages can be classified based on their relative transparency or depth; for instance, German is transparent, though not to the same extent as Spanish, while Japanese is deep, but not as much as Chinese. Arabic, however, can be classified as both shallow (in its formal standards) and deep, considering the variety of sounds in different dialects.

Naturally, the depth of a language evolves from transparent to deeper over time due to the natural process of phonetic change. Periodically, some languages undertake orthographic reforms to align with updated sound patterns, aiming to enhance linguistic foundations and facilitate learning. Other languages adopt a more conservative approach, allowing greater depth to ensure comprehension and maintain a widespread standard among various dialect speakers. This conservatism helps preserve the sounds of numerous dialects and conserves valuable older texts in their original scripts, particularly sacred narratives, and significant literary works.

Balancing orthographic depth is a critical aspect of language planning. Shallow orthography is suitable for languages with smaller speaker populations and less dialectal variation, such as various Caucasian languages and Russian. In contrast, deep orthography is better suited for languages with high diversity and lower mutual intelligibility, such as Kurdish.

Currently, both Kurdish orthographic systems are considered transparent and have not yet developed significant depth. The transparency can be attributed to the relative novelty of these systems (no more than one century old) and their specific adaptation to local contexts.

A system that is implemented locally, rather than universally for all speakers of the language, can perform effectively. However, creating a unified inclusive standard would require greater depth to be as comprehensive as possible and capable of accommodating most, if not all, spoken varieties.

6.2.5 Multiple Orthographic Systems

Kurdish, like some other languages, employs more than one orthographic system simultaneously, specifically Latin and Arabic. This phenomenon –the use of more than one orthographic system for the same language-, known as digraphia, is also observed in languages such as Hindustani, Mandarin, and Persian. However, unlike Kurdish, the unity of these languages is maintained by a common linguistic framework. Despite differences in writing

VI. Phonology & Orthography

systems, they share the same lexicon, syntax, and grammar, even if their alphabets vary.

For instance, Urdu and Hindi use the Arabic-Persian alphabet in Pakistan and the Devanagari script in India, respectively, yet they retain a high degree of mutual intelligibility, making oral communication perfectly clear. Mandarin employs traditional characters in Taiwan, Hong Kong, and Macau, while simplified characters are used in China (since 1949), Singapore (since 1969), and Malaysia (since 1981). Persian is written with the Arabic-Persian alphabet in Iran, Afghanistan, and among overseas communities, and with the Cyrillic script in Tajikistan.

Kurdish, however, has historically been written in various scripts, including Pahlavi, Arabic, Armenian, Cyrillic, and the Yazidi religious alphabet, before settling on the two current systems. The critical distinction for Kurdish is that each orthographic system is associated with a different dialect, influenced by local sociocultural norms, without a unified grammar, syntax, or, to some extent, lexicon. Consequently, Kurdish digraphia is intertwined with diglossia, resulting in distinct ethnolects or sub-languages. This duality may eventually lead to the emergence of entirely separate languages in the future.

6.2.6 Kurdish Orthography

In the period following the Muslim-Arab invasion of Iranshahr, the Pahlavi-speaking homeland, Kurdish, unlike its sister language Persian, did not develop a distinct orthographic system despite being another Pahlavi descendant. The critical reasons for this were:

1. The semi-nomadic lifestyle of the Kurdish tribes, due to environmental circumstances, characterized by seasonal migration, hindered the establishment of dedicated educational institutions, which are essential for developing a prominent education system. Consequently, there was no perceived necessity for a standardized orthography.

2. The inability to establish a significant state that could enforce Kurdish as the official language for administrative purposes.

3. The diminished status of the Kurdish language in comparison to liturgical Arabic led prominent Kurdish scholars to present their literary, religious, and scientific works in Arabic, which had a well-established orthographic discipline.

4. Continuous tribal displacement due to wars and disputes, in addition to environmental factors further obstructed the development of an effective educational system.

5. In a region characterized by ongoing conflicts, the necessity of self-defense has taken precedence, significantly impeding academic pursuits.

VII. Language Segregation

"A language is not just words. It's a culture, a tradition, a unification of a community; a whole history that creates what a community is. It's all embodied in a language."

Noam Chomsky (*)

Until the turn of the 20th century, the Kurdish language faced significant neglect, struggling for survival throughout its painful history. No formal standard was developed, nor was the language considered by authors and scientists for their works. Consequently, when formal standards were needed for administrative purposes in the newly independent country of Iraq, the diverse vernaculars sufficed only for day-to-day oral use and regional communication. However, as colloquial language falls short in conveying high-level or complex ideas, there was an urgent need for modern linguistic standards.

At that time, where no formal dialect existed, the immediate solution involved hastily preparing local vocabulary and syntax for spontaneous use. Formal Sorani was crafted based on the dialect of a small group of speakers in Sulaymaniyah to expedite the process. This approach provided a quick solution but compromised the intelligibility of the majority of Kurdish speakers. Similarly, the Kurmanji orthography was modified under the influence of the Turkish writing system, entirely disregarding the earlier efforts in developing Sorani, and creating a different grammar and vocabulary.

---

* From the movie 'We Still Live Here: Âs Nutayuneân

These developments resulted in the Kurdish language being divided into two main branches—Sorani and Kurmanji—making mutual intelligibility more challenging and rendering the identity of the Kurdish language controversial. Furthermore, this division repelled other dialects from the linguistic mainstream. As a result, these uncoordinated efforts propagated the concept of ethnolect division rather than mere linguistic dialects. From a sociolinguistic perspective, this is considered a step towards the emergence of new ethnicities from the weakening Kurdish identity, akin to the evolution of Spanish and Italian from Vulgar Latin in the 16th century.

7.1 Linguistic Barriers

Communication barriers hinder the dynamic evolution of a society. Today, the Kurdish nation faces internal communication challenges, including diglossia, digraphia, and the current geopolitical situation, often referred to as the "curse of geography".

7.1.1 Diglossia

The majority of the world's living languages comprise various dialects across different regions and communities. Typically, these languages adopt one formal dialect for purposes such as education and media, which may or may not be the spoken variety of any particular group. The use of two different dialects within a single language for distinct functions—one formal and the other colloquial for everyday communication—is known as diglossia (Schiffman, 2003, p. 116). The term was introduced by the German scholar Karl Krumbacher, who discussed diglossia in both Greek and Arabic in 1903 (Benjamin, 1992, p. 3). The concept gained widespread attention after sociolinguist Charles Ferguson (1959, p 325) defined the term as follows:

VII. Language Segregation

"Two varieties of a language exist[ing] side by side with each having a definite role to play."

A group of people from Baghdad, for instance, speaks a specific variety of Arabic distinct from the Arabic spoken in Tunisia or Kuwait. When Kuwaitis communicate with Tunisians, they often approximate comprehension by borrowing words from a common dialect, such as Standard Arabic or the colloquial Cairo dialect, which has gained popularity through the widespread dissemination of Egyptian movies and TV dramas. For formal communication, however, they use the uniform standard dialect 'AlFusha' (الفصحى), a formal and religious variety not natively spoken by any Arabic-speaking group in their daily lives.

Another example of a strongly diglossic language is Chinese, which is not a monolithic linguistic entity but rather an umbrella term that includes all variations of the Han Chinese language(s) (Liu K., 2018). Since 1912, numerous phonetic schemes have been developed to facilitate the standardization of a unified spoken variety. In 1932, finally, the Beijing dialect was officially recognized as the basis for the national spoken standard.

For each language, the standard variety, referred to as the *High variety*, abbreviated in linguistic studies as 'H,' is restricted by linguistic rules that are usually resistant to change over time and often serve as a bridge language for better intelligibility in communication involving multiple dialects. The Low variety, abbreviated as 'L', however, is flexible, tolerates changes in word meanings, and is subject to unplanned modification over time.

Compared to Arabic, Italian, and Chinese, Kurdish has not yet developed a single unified High variety to serve as a linguistic bridge across its Low varieties. Thus, according to the definition of diglossia, the Sorani dialect is not diglossic due to its orthographic transparency, nor is Kurmanji. However, Kurdish can be considered highly diglossic, or more accurately, *multiglossic*, due to its multiple varieties with low interdialectal intelligibility. Consequently, speakers may communicate, reluctantly, through another language.

7.1.2 Digraphia

This term refers to the use of more than one writing system for the same language. Many languages around the world are digraphic such as Serbian which is written in Latin and Cyrillic; some others are trigraphic like Japanese which is written in three systems: hiragana, katakana, and kanji.

Diachronic digraphia exists when different writing systems are adopted at different periods of time, examples of this are Turkish (written in Arabic before being changed to Latin in 1928), Uzbek, Moldavian, and Turkman. These nations have switched from Cyrillic to Latin following the collapse of the Soviet Union.

Synchronous digraphia, however, is the coexistence of more than one writing system at the same time for the same language.

From the fall of Pahlavi until the early twentieth century, Kurdish had been written mainly in the Arabic formal system, before the birth of Sorani-Arabic, and Persian; hence by Cyrillic and Latin during the Soviet Union in Armenia and the *Krasni Kurdistan* administrative unit of Azerbaijan SSR between 1923 and 1929. It is not the only language in the Middle East to adopt synchronous digraphia; Azerbaijani (Arabic in Iran and Latin in Azerbaijan), Persian (Arabic in Iran and Afghanistan, and Cyrillic in Tajikistan), and the Urdo-Hindi (Arabic-Persian in Pakistan and Devanagari system in India); yet the difference is that these languages do not associate the different scripts to different varieties. Kurdish is the only language that adopts two synchronous orthographies for two varieties that do not share the same standards for grammar or spelling. The conjunction of diglossia and digraphia of two varieties that are separated by international borders by some means denotes a coexistence of two distinct sub-languages, Sorani and Kurmanji, rather than a single integrated language.

VII. Language Segregation

7.1.4 Kurdish Multiglossia

Compared to other diglossic languages such as Arabic, Persian, Chinese, and Norwegian, Kurdish faces significant challenges, and is the most venerable among all. Unlike Kurdish, the extremely conservative Arabic employs a universal standard to be used in formal communication, which is unique and official across more than twenty multi-dialectal countries. This standard preserves linguistic unity through its unique lexicon and grammar despite the less intelligible colloquial dialects. Similarly, Persian, which is both diglossic and digraphic, maintains national heritage and linguistic unity by using a single formal standard.

Languages are not ranked by the abundance of cognates or grammatical variations. Instead, the presence of numerous exact synonyms, diverse spelling and grammar rules, and the absence of a common formal variety result in adverse effects, including:

- Aggravated intelligibility.
- Creation of sub-ethnic sentiments and reduced interest in socializing with speakers of other dialects.
- Increased burden on the learning process.
- Reduced language status.
- Diminished international presence of the language.

In contrast to other diglossic languages, Kurdish multiglossia does not enrich the language nor elevate its status, rather, it is merely an element of linguistic fragmentation.

7.2 Sub-Ethnic Fragments

Due to lexical and orthographical divisions across vast geopolitically isolated regions, Kurdish is linguistically considered a disintegrated language. These grammatical and scripting divergences render the two major dialects more akin to separate languages with similarities rather than merely hard-to-communicate dialects. This division critically undermines the unity of the language, weakening the psychological bonds within the nation's cultural fabric. In the long term, this linguistic fragmentation may foreshadow more pronounced ethnic variations and psychological splits within the population, fostering a sense of sub-ethnicity.

The impact of this linguistic cleavage is evident in the short-term future, as it psychologically insinuates an imperceptible cross-national division. This division is not limited to the two main dialects but extends to others such as Laki, Gorani, and Zaza, who may feel alienated and driven to seek distinct identities apart from the collective national symbol of unity, the Kurdish language. This situation has prompted some influential figures to advocate the founding of formal grammar systems for other dialects, such as Zaza in the north and Faili in the south, suggesting further sub-ethnic identities. These efforts have been subtly encouraged by Turkish and Iraqi authorities.

Official efforts by Turkey, particularly after the ultra-nationalist coup of 1980, aimed to develop Zazaki into a full-fledged literary language, aiming to separate Zaza and Kurmanji although these initiatives have been largely unsuccessful (Keskin, 2017). In Iran, dialects are often referred to as 'languages,' زبان blurring the distinction between language and dialect and imparting a sense of linguistic independence to the Kurdish dialects.

7.2.1 Purism

One of the major obstacles to building a homogeneous language is ethnolinguistic purism, the practice of defining varieties based on a scale of ethnic purity or of intrinsicality for cultural or historical reasons. Purism may emerge from social or economic circumstances or be deliberately planned as part of a language ideology.

The most common types of planned purism are:

1. **Archaizing purism**: Maintains an old variety, as seen in Arabic, which preserves the form of the language's golden age across generations.

VII. Language Segregation

2. **Reformist purism**: Removes older styles or foreign loanwords, exemplified by the Turkish state's efforts under Ataturk to eliminate Persian and Arabic loanwords.

3. **Elitist purism**: Associates the formal variety with the standards and vocabulary used by the elite (Thomas, 1991, pp. 75-83).

4. **Ethnographic purism**: Grants superior prestige to one variety over others within the same language, such as the selection of the Beijing dialect as the formal standard in China (Li, 2004).

However, when a language lacks a single formal variety, as with Kurdish, ethnographic purism weakens national affiliations and sentiments among speakers of varieties deemed less pure, such as those other than Sorani in Kurdistan and other than Kurmanji in Turkey. The linguistic disintegration resulting from the absence of a unique standard contributes significantly to the entrenchment of this phenomenon within the social and cultural norms of the Kurdish community.

7.2.2 Sociocultural Development

Idioms, poems, metaphors, proverbs, and other influential socio-psychological expressions and traditions evolve over time, marking social developments within distinct regional contexts. Vocabulary evolves and changes alongside cultural advancements, with some phrases fading out and new ones emerging, often classified by the decades in which they appear. Consequently, languages continuously update themselves, modifying their lexicon, grammar, and phonetic patterns at varying rates and levels of adaptability. However, Kurdish culture is notably conservative, characterized by its perceptible purity.

One clear indication of the conservative nature of Kurdish culture is its preservation of the Pahlavi linguistic lexicon, despite significant phonological changes. Compared to Persian, Kurdish has maintained morphological purity. However, due to the lack of a dedicated orthography, it has experienced considerable phonological bias, which contributed to the emergence of Kurdish as a distinct language and its dialects. Without this phonological evolution, Kurdish might not have developed as a separate language, and speakers may have continued to use Pahlavi across the Iranian plateau, from the Mediterranean Sea to the outskirts of Pakistan. Several factors have contributed to lexical sustainability and phonological passivity, as discussed below.

7.2.2.1 Environment

The environment plays a significant role in originating phonological changes, altering the distribution of phonemes, and modifying the acoustic structure of speech (Howell, 2008). While the rugged mountainous terrain and impassable winter passages of the region offer protection from invasions, they also limit the movement of tribes, reduce mutual contact, and strain internal communication among geographically dispersed communities.

Harsh winters prompt migrations to warmer valleys (migration of *Garmian*) and back to the mountains in summer (migration of *Koystan*), creating a semi-nomadic lifestyle that lacks the stability necessary for cultural prosperity. The protective yet harsh nature of the Zagros terrain imposes isolation on the inhabitants' culture, contributing to the divergence and reshaping of the Kurdish dialects. This environment hinders the growth of cities and the establishment of academic institutions that could protect linguistic characteristics and unity.

Different regions exhibit varying co-articulatory behaviors (Recasens, 1999). For example, the pronunciation of plosive phonemes may require easing air restriction and allowing wider space inside the vocal tract especially when articulated at higher volumes. Unlike in dense urban centers, louder conversations often occur in rural areas with low population density. Phonemes like /b/ are more easily produced when the mouth is open (lips are kept apart), leading to shifts toward /v/ or /w/. Similar shifts occur with phonemes such as /d/, /m/, and /n/. The Pahlavi word 'Ab' /'aːb/ (water) has shifted to /'aːv/ and /'aːw/ in recent dialects; similarly, the Arabic word 'Salam' has changed to 'Slav' and 'Slaw' for the same reasons. In addition to phonetic and phonological changes, the environment also affects grammar and vocabulary.

As the evolving lifestyle in the vast Kurdish-speaking region has led to gradual changes in articulation habits, resulting in current

VII. Language Segregation

phonological differences, words have been affected by various phonetic deviations across speakers. Isolated tribes that lost strong communication ties with others were more exposed to phonetic biases. Different articulation habits, such as the positioning of the tongue and lips, among groups of speakers have redistributed phonemes, especially the finals, such as the labiodental 'V' and the labio-velar approximant 'W'. This significant difference between the two major dialects, Sorani and Kurmanji, although not affecting semantics, underlies changes in the pronunciation of words such as:

Sor.	*Sound*	Kurm.	*Sound*	Eng.
Aw (ئاو)	/'aːw/	Av	/'aːv/	Water
Şiwan (شوان)	/ʃɪwaːn/	Şivan	/ʃɪvaːn/	Shepherd
Nîw (نیو)	/slaw/	Nîv	/njv/	Half
Awyn (ئەوین)	/æwˈɪjn/	Evîn	/ævˈɪjn/	Love

The word for 'night' in Kurdish illustrates this divergence: the Kurmanji "Shev" (Şev) /ʃev/ and the Sorani "Shew" (شەو) /ʃeʊ/ both trace back to the Pahlavi 'Shab' /ʃeb/. Both forms are accepted by the speakers without any judgment of correctness.

By crafting a formal variety, Kurdish could have preserved its phonological structure and unified grammar, which would have mitigated dialectal rifts and linguistic branching.

7.2.2.2 Religion

Following the defeat of the Sasanian Empire in the seventh century, Islam successfully proselytized the majority of the Kurdish-speaking population. Historically, this religion endorsed Arabic as a sacred language for practicing rituals. This superstratum status granted to Arabic for the last fourteen centuries significantly contributed to the marginalization of Kurdish. As the lingua franca of the vastly expanded Muslim empire, Arabic was the sole option for scholars, essential for politicians, and encouraged for philosophical and scientific studies. Kurdish descendants, such as Ibn Khalikan, Abu Huzaifa Al-Dainoori, and the prominent musician Zariab Al-Mousili, utilized Arabic for their production. Even the Ayyubid dynasty, which ruled Kurdistan in the medieval period and extended their power to the Levant and Egypt, adopted Arabic over their original Kurdish for religious reasons.

Living under the influence of another language and being excluded from sociocultural development further impoverished Kurdish literature. Thus, the rudimentary usage and confinement to oral communication left Kurdish susceptible to constant phonetic divergence, inevitably resulting in the current linguistic fragmentation.

7.2.2.3 Wars and Invasions

Settling in the heart of the ancient world for centuries, the inhabitants of Mesopotamia, particularly those near the rich water resources, adopted a defensive mentality to maintain their settlements, culture, and language. They developed a self-defense attitude, utilizing strategic battlegrounds and mountain hideouts for survival. This tendency towards isolation for safety purposes reduced linguistic exchange among Kurdish-speaking groups, which gradually led to dialectal divergence, including the loss of common words, biases in pronunciation, and the evolution of local vocabularies.

Additionally, invaders who settled in the area as foreign forces imposed direct bans on the use of Kurdish aiming to suppress the distinct culture—a process known as Turkification, Arabization, and to some extent, Persification. Beginning in the seventh century and continuing until the thirteenth, when Pahlavi was deemed the language of infidelity (Zoroastrianism), the region underwent extensive Arabization under the banner of Islamification. However, following the fall of Abbasid Baghdad in 1258, linguistic constraints were eased, but the language had lost its connection to its roots, and new languages (modern Persian, Kurdish, Pashto, and Balochi) had already evolved with distinct characteristics.

In the modern era, especially since the turn of the twentieth century, intensive Turkification occurred in the north (Turkey and Azerbaijan), Arabization in the south (Syria and Iraq), and Persianization under the Pahlavi dynasty and the Islamic Revolution. Furthermore, the semi-autonomous local states established during

VII. Language Segregation

periods of weak imperial control were often mutually uncooperative and engaged in conflicts. Consequently, political instability and tribal customs fostered further isolation and weakened communication processes among the population groups.

IIX. Kurdish Language Strategy

> *"Language is legislation, speech is its code. We do not see the power which is in speech because we forget that all speech is a classification and that all classifications are oppressive."*
>
> Roland Barthes

The dominant rule in linguistics is the rule that says there is no rule in linguistics, not for grammar nor for word coining. Languages are formed as habitual practices among speaker populations growing conventionally and independently of each other. This diversity underscores the distinct character inherent in each language, having its own set of regulations that randomly and independently grow, widening the linguistic gap and aggravating understandability. Yet at the same time, it grants linguists a degree of flexibility to amend principles based on social, cultural, and religious demands. Linguists can regulate grammar, adjust semantics, and add words to their vocabulary. The formal Sorani, based on this fact, developed an orthographic presentation of phonemes a century ago based on the opinions of Mula Sa'ed Kaban. A decade later, the 'rule of no rules' allowed the evolution of the formal Kurmanji by Mir Celadet Bedirxan. Thus, a unified formal Kurdish, based on this flexibility, could have been practically formed provided that the founders of both standards had cooperated on a single project; moreover, a single standard dialect is feasibly achievable in the future if the contemporary socio-political facets are thoroughly contemplated. The linguistic unification meets the preconditions for success, given that an authorized academy is established. A fundamental strategy may not be confined to a corpus solution but also be extended as a socio-linguistic project with a futuristic perspective that contributes to geopolitical, economic, and cultural advancements. However, objectives may not be achieved without inspiring an influential language ideology.

The superstratum is principal for national prosperity, taking into consideration the role of language as a national identity, and the value of the language is reflected in the value of the speaking population.

8.1 Struggle for Identity

A cursory examination reveals that the Middle East has yet to fully transcend the historical phase of national conflicts. The prevailing mindset in this region involves each group striving to establish historical ties to the land – that is, to legitimize their claims of ownership. These efforts are shaped by the Bedouin mentality, characterized by a nomadic lifestyle devoid of permanent attachment to any specific land. This mentality has resulted in ongoing disputes over territory as these groups have attempted to settle in contested areas. Beyond the Arab-Israeli hostilities and Allegations on Kurdish lands, various small religious minorities also continue to strive for recognition of their ancient roots. This pervasive debate remains heavily influenced by the implications of a nomadic lifestyle, with each group attempting to reset or even distort historical evidence with suggestions or unrealistic claims, aiming to prove the antiquity of one nation over another. This form of arbitration is used to establish the legitimacy of settlement in a specific geographical area.

In such an atmosphere, much of the historical and Kurdological research seeking to define national identity examines the Kurds primarily from an anthropological perspective, often neglecting their cultural and linguistic heritage. Researchers have concentrated on identifying the origins of the earliest tribes that formed the initial Kurdish communities only to prove that Kurds have been living long enough. While these studies are enthusiastically received as evidence of the Kurds' deep historical presence in the region, there has been a notable lack of equivalent efforts to analyze the concurrent social factors and the impact of diachronic linguistic developments. The

IIX. Kurdish Language Strategy

emphasis on politics and history relegated language, the most crucial element of national identity, to a lower priority. Consequently, the Kurdish language did not receive adequate planning or attention to linguistic strategy.

8.1.1 Philological Rooting

Given that the Kurdish lexicon is inherited and phonetically biased from older varieties, tracing the diachronic derivation of a dialectally biased morpheme is best achieved by referring to these older varieties. For instance, to find a single cognate for the Kurm. 'Înê' and Sor. 'Heyni' (English: 'Friday'), one can refer to older dialects like Gorani/Zaza, where it appears in various phonetic forms such as "*enne, yene, yenne*, and *éne*".(*) A unified lexicon spelling can be selected based on similarity to the cognate in other dialects. If the older form does not provide a suitable alternative, the common morpheme 'eyn' found in both 'Înê' and 'Heyni' can guide the selection of a substitute grapheme to replace the initial letters 'Î' and 'N'. For example, in English, 'Friday' refers to the day of Frigg, the goddess of motherhood. Frigg in ancient Germanic mythology corresponds to the Arian goddess of fertility 'n'hyt' or Enahita. It is possible that 'Înê' and 'Heyni' are derived from 'ena', as an abbreviated form of Enahyta. (†)

An alternative philological approach offers a practical suggestion. Sister languages such as Luri, Persian, Pashtun, Baluchi, and other Iranic-origin languages may serve as valuable resources for borrowing words. Linguistic consanguinity ensures semantically closer cognates that are easier to represent orthographically and adapt phonologically. For example, 'Înê' and 'Heyni' may have originated from the Pahlavi word 'Adine', still in use in Persian, considering the modern Kurdish tendency to omit the phoneme /d/.

In general, Kurdish is morphologically conservative while being phonetically tolerant—it updates vocally while preserving the original morphemes. In contrast, the sister language Persian, due to

---

* https://glosbe.com/en/zza/friday
† https://glosbe.com/pal/en/%CA%BEn%CA%BEhyt

its advanced orthography, has managed to preserve morphemes phonologically closer to their origins.

8.1.2 Kurdification

In the context of the prevailing contemporary cosmopolitan culture, linguistic purity no longer exists, and every language incorporates loanwords into its vocabulary. Kurdish, in particular, has experienced multiple linguistic invasions, with each language leaving some foreign imprints. However, foreign words have often been rejected or Kurdified. Recently, Sorani has managed to resist strong cognates by Kurdifying terms such as 'Football' to "تۆپی پێ" (Topi pê), 'Journalism' to "ڕۆژنامەگەری" (Rojhnamagary), and 'Airplane' to "فڕۆکە" (Faroka). Some loanwords borrowed in a particular dialect have no presence in others, such as the Turkish words in Sorani, "Kız" (Sor. کچ "Kich" - Eng. Girl), "Bardak" (Eng. Cup), and "Kalabalik" (Eng. Crowded).

For the purpose of linguistic unity, loanwords that have replaced Kurdish equivalents in a specific dialect, thereby reducing mutual intelligibility, can be Kurdified. For example:

- "Kich" (Eng. Girl, Daughter): has a common Kurdish equivalent "Dot," still used in the dialects of Kurmanji, Gorani, and Pahlawani.

- "Berdagh" (Eng. Cup, Mug): has a common Kurdish equivalent "Piyala."

- "Dukan" (Eng. Shop): can be Kurdified to "Faroushgah," which contains the morphemes "Faroush" (Sell) from the stem "فرۆشتن" (Selling) and the suffix "Gah" or "Ga" (Place). This word is already in use in Eastern Kurdistan.

In addition to vocabulary, syntax Kurdification can also contribute positively to unification. An example of dialectal syntactic disharmony is the use of the preposition 'in' as a suffix in Sorani ("da" / "دا") and Kurmanji ("de"), borrowed from the Turkish "de," while the Kurdish equivalents "li" (Kurmanji) and "le" (Sorani) already exist. Notably, the preposition suffix 'de' is redundant in colloquial usage and is used mainly in formal communication.

IIX. Kurdish Language Strategy

For instance, the sentence "*The book is in the library*" is syntactically coined as:

- Sorani: "Ktebeke le ktebkhane**da**ye" (كتێبەکە لە کتێبخانە_دا_یە).
- Kurmanji: "Pirtûk di pirtûkxaneyê **de** ye".
- Turkish: "Kitap kütüphane**de**".

While the suffix is semantically essential in Turkish, it can be dropped in both Kurmanji and Sorani without affecting the sentence's meaning.

Kurdification is an integral part of a language ideology that promotes the stratum status of a superstratum. If words are coined under an authorized linguistic academy, Kurdification may contribute to the process of unification. However, since some commonly used international terms are associated with precise concepts, linguistic purism should treat international scientific vocabulary leniently to avoid conceptual overlap (if Kurdified)with the meaning of the native cognate -that is Kurdification is not a replacement for the unification project; in addition to enhancing the language stratum, its main significance lies in contributing toward dialectal leveling.

8.1.3 Dialectal Leveling

When circumstances allow groups of speakers of different dialects to engage in long-term contact, these dialects mutually influence each other, approximating vocabularies and grammar habits. Sustained communication among different dialect speakers raises the level of common intelligibility in an involuntary process known as *dialectal leveling*. This process is defined by the Canadian linguist Claire Lefebvre (1998, p. 41) as:

"*refers to the reduction of variation between dialects of the same language in situations where speakers of these dialects are brought together.*"

Dialectal leveling, triggered by contact between speakers of different dialects, is observed in most modern languages. Social upheaval, major cities attracting trade and inhabitants from different regions, and the emergence of Creole languages contribute to this phenomenon. In the last century, particularly after the influential expansion of common arts such as movies and TV drama, and more recently the social media revolution, dialectal leveling has accelerated rapidly on a wider scale. Dialect-specific vocabulary becomes exposed to others; for instance, the Kurmanji word 'Berxwedan' (pronounced 'Barkhudan') has become commonly understood among Sorani speakers alongside the native cognates 'Raparin' (ڕاپەڕین) and "Bargri kirdin" (بەرگری کردن) due to increased media influence.

However, dialectal leveling in Kurdish is generally slower than in neighboring languages due to the burdensome transportation and mobility restrictions imposed on citizens across the international borders that divide the Kurdish-speaking region.

The divergence and multitude of varieties do not enrich a language; rather, they burden it with redundant cognates, lowering mutual intelligibility, reducing stratum, weakening dialectal liaisons, and consequently leading to a growing sense of ethnolects. For example, the word 'city' appears in two forms: Sorani 'Shar' (شار) and Kurmanji 'Bajar', both of which are synonymous without contributing to semantic feasibility. It only enriches Kurdish when connoting different concepts, similar to 'city' and 'town' in English. In general, having semantically identical words may not be considered harmful if they coexist within the same variety, as the less popular term may fade over time. However, it becomes problematic if each word is attributed to a specific dialect, creating an atmosphere of conflicting ethnolects.

To conclude, language leveling is a strategic means that, if well-planned, can contribute to the better use of Kurdish.

8.2 Practical Solutions

Today, most living integrated languages have, at various points in history, experienced survival struggles and dialectal disintegration.

IIX. Kurdish Language Strategy

Consequently, Kurdish can benefit from examining the diverse solutions employed by other languages and selecting the most appropriate example for its modernization reforms. Unification instances provide numerous strategies for adopting a single common dialect for formal use. The unification strategies include selecting an existing dialect, creating a new standard, diachronically referring to the proto-language, and adopting harmonized multi-formal varieties. Each of these solutions has been successfully implemented by at least one of today's living languages. Yet, the ultimate enforcement step is primarily an administrative decision dependent on state policy rather than a cultural issue that intellectuals and scholars can definitively resolve.

8.2.1 Selecting an Existing Variety

This solution is the most common globally, typically arising under exceptional historical circumstances, such as post-war or civil conflict resolutions. For instance, the unification of the Italian language resulted from the national unification of Italy, achieved by capturing Rome in 1871. Similarly, the unification of Germany in the same year led to the final stage of German language unification, culminating in the publication of the first unified German dictionary by Konrad Duden in 1880.

A dialect may be selected for standardization based on various criteria, including the population of its speakers (e.g., Chinese Mandarin), the historical depth of its standard form (e.g., formal Arabic), the richness of its literary tradition (e.g., Italian Tuscany), or its dialectal prestige (e.g., French Parisian). Choosing an existing variety can help avoid the extensive time and effort required for lengthy technical linguistic discourse and the necessity of translating publications into the newly adopted standard form.

Each of the main four Kurdish varieties holds the potential to establish a formal standard for unification: Kurmanji, with the highest number of speakers; Sorani, with the most extensive publication history; Gorani/Zaza, as the oldest written form; and Pahlawani, the closest to ancient Pahlavi.

However, the primary obstacle to selecting and generalizing a specific dialect is the need for an authoritative resolution, which is unlikely in the short term due to current political circumstances. Another significant challenge is the phenomenon of dialectal purism.

Purism: The Scale of Kurdishness

The principles of modern nationalism strive for a unified, indivisible nation, transforming society from a tribal configuration to a cohesive group of citizens defined by a singular ethnic identity. In this context, a Kurd is recognized solely as a Kurd, irrespective of sub-identities such as tribe, religion, or dialect; every Kurdish descendant is considered equal in their Kurdishness. However, the Kurdish nationalist movement has not fully realized this objective nor cultivated sufficient public awareness to develop modern nationalistic ideals, wherein national identity takes precedence over sub-ethnic, religious, and sectarian orientations.

The most evident reason for this shortfall is the failure to establish an independent state, particularly after World War I, which not only hindered the formation of a fundamental political structure but also the development of social concepts necessary for a unified and integrated social fabric. This deficiency is evident today in the persistence of premodern national ideologies, where sub-languages and sub-ethnic sentiments continue to be significant aspects of the Kurdish identity (Kreyenbroek & Sperl, 2005, pp. 35-36).

Purism, a set of sentiments predating modern nationalism, classifies groups within a nation based on ethnic and linguistic purity. In the absence of modern nationalist ideals and strong linguistic unity, purism has emerged as a sociocultural phenomenon influencing Kurdish self-identification. Thus, the perceived purity of Kurdishness varies among groups, with some considered closer to pure Kurdishness than others, especially those linguistically intertwined with neighboring cultures.

The scale of Kurdishness is primarily based on dialect and accent; the clearer and more prominent the dialect, the higher its position on the scale. Additionally, the historical involvement of speakers in the national struggle, cultural traditions (e.g., clothing and cuisine), religion, and geographic proximity are other factors influencing

IIX. Kurdish Language Strategy

Kurdishness. For example, due to linguistic barriers, a Sorani speaker may be perceived as having a lower degree of Kurdishness compared to a Kurmanji speaker, in areas where "Kurdish" and "Kurmanji" are often used interchangeably.

Selecting an existing dialect for linguistic unification is inevitably affected by the scale of Kurdishness and may face resistance from speakers of other dialects. Strategic linguistic planning might consider leveling the dialectal stratum among all Kurdish speakers to facilitate any unification process as more practical than selecting a single dialect. L. O. Fossum (1919, p 3) highlighted the prevalence of purism in Kurdish culture, demonstrating the challenge of selecting a specific dialect over others.

"To discover the best Kurdish among these many dialects is not an easy task. Lerch states that it is useless to ask the Kurds as to which dialect is the best, for every Kurd claims that his own dialect is the purest and best. The linguists themselves have a tendency to give the same kind of answer: The dialect they study the most becomes the purest and best 'for them."

8.2.1.1 Sorani

The first significant period of development is linked to the rise of the Baban Emirate (1649-1851), which was governed by Sulaymaniyah. During this time, the city's dialect gained popularity in literature, with many poets contributing to its enrichment and solidifying its presence among other Kurdish varieties.

During the period of Ottoman rule, authorities propagated the belief that any attempt to modify Arabic letters to suit the Kurdish writing style was blasphemous and punishable by death. (*) This forewarning was intended to thwart any serious effort to create a Kurdish writing system, despite the fact that the Ottoman language itself was written in a modified Arabic (Persian) script. Consequently, pioneering efforts to establish a Kurdish writing system began in earnest only after the fall of the Ottoman Empire. The major work to associate modern Kurdish (Sorani) with the Arabic-Persian script was

---

* https://kurdishacademy.org/?page_id=197

introduced by L. O. Fossum in 1919. He presented a 32-letter alphabet modeled on Persian, complete with detailed examples of consonants, vowels, and diphthongs. (Fossum, 1919, p 3) Saeed Sidqi Kaban, a native Kurdish speaker and graduate of religious Quranic schools, challenged the Ottoman claims in his book titled *Gulzar* in 1920. Although he was unable to publish, he incorporated its contents into his later work, *Mukhtasar Sarf u Nahu i Kurdi* (The Concise Kurdish Inflection and Grammar), published in 1928. Kaban eventually modified the Persian-Arabic script to create a writing system based on the Sulaymaniyah dialect, emphasizing various parts of speech using Arabic grammar as a model. Another significant contributor to Kurdish grammar and the writing system was Colonel Tawfiq Wahby. He added diacritics to the modified Arabic-Persian script, using single or combined characters for each phoneme, including vowels. His book دەستوورى زمانى کوردى (Grammar of the Kurdish Language), published in 1929, was praised by E. McCarus (1958, p. 3), who described it as follows:

> *"This is an excellent description of Sulaymaniyah Kurdish by a native speaker of that dialect. The grammar is prescriptive in nature, attempting to 'purify' the language of its non-Kurdish elements."*

After the First World War when the radical changes in power in the Middle East provided an opportunity for Kurdish to be formalized for modern administrative purposes. The British mandate in Iraq assigned Colonel Tawfiq Wahby, a linguistics enthusiast, to develop a standard form of Kurdish that could meet the modern requirements of administration.

> *"In 1923, The venerable Iraqi Ministry of Education commissioned me to write a book on Kurdish language grammar. After arduous effort and long continuous work, I wrote the book, titled 'Destouri Zimani Kurdi', published the first part and some of the second in 1929-1930."* (*)

---

* Wahbi, Tawfiq (1956). Ch 1. Part 1

"في عام 1923 كلفتني وزارة المعارف العراقية الجليلة ان اضع كتابا في قواعد اللغة الكردية، وبعد جهد مضن وعمل طويل تواصل وضعت كتاب 'ده ستوري زماني كوردي'، ونشرت الجزء الاول منه وقسما من الجزء الثاني في عام 1929-1930، لكن ظروفا خاصة حالت دون نشر ما تبقى من الكتاب".

IIX. Kurdish Language Strategy

Today, Sorani, officially recognized by the Kurdistan Regional Government (KRG) and Iraqi authorities as the formal standard of Kurdish, has established a rich vocabulary and relatively precise semantics through decades of use.

The advance of formal Sorani in the region of South Kurdistan has been deeply associated with formulating sociocultural beliefs and social superstructure, building up monolingualism in Kurdish society manifested by the expansion of literature, print, and visual media production. By 2014, the growing number of satellite television stations exceeded 30 that is in addition to around 780 print-media publications among them 5 daily newspapers according to the leader of the Kurdistan Journalists Syndicate Azad Shaikh Younis, commented in his interview with Aljazeera Television station. (*)

Alphabet Systems

By the turn of the twentieth century, the variety was associated with the Persian writing system, which is based on Arabic alphabets augmented with letters representing the Iranic-specific sounds missing in Arabic: پ, چ, ژ, گ, and ڤ for G, J /ʒ/, Ch /tʃ/, P, and V, respectively. This system was adopted by the Kingdom of Kurdistan, which emerged in Sulaymaniyah (1921-1925), officially used from the top administrative communications, including the written correspondence of King Mahmoud to the education system under the ministry of Major General Mustafa Yamulki (1866-1936).

The major Soranification efforts were led by Tawfiq Wahbi based on the efforts of Sa'ed Sidiq Kaban. Aiming to develop a phonemic system, new letters were introduced 'ڕ' /ɾ/, 'ڵ' /ɫ/, 'وو' /u/, and the diphthong 'ێ' /ɪə/. Influenced by the way the Latin system represents short vowels, he replaced the Arabic diacritics '—ؘ' /ə/, '—ؙ' /ʊ/, '—ؚ' /ɪ/ by the letters 'ە' ,'و', and 'ی'. Col.

Wahbi in his quest to build a transparent writing system that accurately reflects pronunciation, later wrote:

---

* Azad Shaikh Younis. الإعلام-بكردستان-العراق-طموح-جامح [The media in Kurdistan, a wild ambition]. "aljazeera.net". 12 Jan 2014
https://www.aljazeera.net/news/2014/1/12/الإعلام-بكردستان-العراق-طموح-جامح

"At the outset, I encountered a significant challenge in utilizing Arabic letters to represent Kurdish sounds. Enumerating all the Kurdish phonetic elements using Arabic script and determining appropriate diacritics required considerable effort, particularly during the development of the grammatical framework." (*)

In evaluating Wahbi's work, it is evident that his focus was primarily on the phonological aspect, using a sample of sounds from a localized area and attempting to generalize them into a phonemic language. This approach overlooked the rich variety of phonemes and pronunciations among the broader population outside the Sulaymaniyah region. Overemphasizing a local phonological structure at the expense of orthographic opacity effectively creates a new local language rather than a comprehensive national standard.

Currently, Sorani, with its extensive publications and rich literary heritage compared to other dialects, is a strong candidate for a unified national variety. However, achieving a higher degree of practicality necessitates orthographic and grammatical enhancements. The major modifications include:

- ✓ Abandoning the current writing system in favor of the Latin alphabet to facilitate learning in other Kurdish-speaking regions.

- ✓ Addressing the pronunciation bias of phonemes across dialects by adopting a single grapheme for interchanging phonemes. For example, unifying the spelling of Sorani /ʊ/, Kurmanji /v/, and Gorani 'w' /ʊ/ and 'Kh' /x/; enabling all speakers to read words in a unified spelling, such as standardizing the spelling of Sorani 'Aw' and Kurmanji 'Av'.

- ✓ Implementing syntactic and grammatical enhancements where necessary, such as addressing dialectal differences in the transitive past tense.

---

* Wahbi, Tawfiq (1956). Ch 1. Part 1.

"ومشكلة اخرى جابهتني منذ ان بدأت، وهي كتابة اللغة الكردية بالحروف العربية، فكان علي ان اقوم بتثبيت اصوات اللغة الكردية وحركاتها. وان تثبيت هذه الاصوات والحركات جميعها بالحروف العربية مع وضع اشارات خاصة لها وتدوين الكتابة بها، اقتضاني جهدا غير قليل، بذلته في اثناء تدوين قواعد اللغة"

IIX. Kurdish Language Strategy

8.2.1.2 Kurmanji

It is the primary variety in terms of the speaker population, merit that alone positions it as a strong candidate for selection as the unifying standard. Additionally, it is the only dialect spoken across all Kurdish regions, including the four major areas, the remote enclave of Khurasan, and the former Soviet communities in Russia, Azerbaijan, Armenia, Georgia, and Kazakhstan. The use of this variety has been increasing over the past decades due to the relative relaxation of restrictions by Turkish authorities and the growing activities of Kurdish media in Western Europe, in addition to the formal use in the semi-independent territory in Northern Syria.

Kurmanji is the dialect of the sacred Ezedi scriptures, "*Meṣḥefa Reş*" and "*Kitêba Cilwe*". Its sanctity and spiritual stature provide a sustainable foundation for formalization, similar to Arabic, Latin, and Hebrew. There have also been attempts to create a linguistic distinction between vernacular Kurmanji and what has been termed Ezediky as a formal standard to maintain religious values, thereby enhancing linguistic standards. Owing to their nationalist inclination, prominent Ezedi figures have long contributed to the Kurdish language in fields such as art and literature. The first state-supported Kurdish theater was launched by Ezedi Kurds of Elegez in Armenia in 1937 when the language was still banned in Turkey and Syria (Sözeri & Konak, 2022). The first Kurdish novel, "Şьvane Kyrmança" (The Kurmanji Shepherd), was written by Arab Shamilov in 1929 and published by the Armenian Kurdish publishing house "Nəşra Hykymətə Şewra Ermənistane." The first Kurdish movie, titled "Zarê," produced by the Soviet film company Armenkino, was directed by Hamo Beknazarian in 1926. (*) Both A. Shamilov and H. Benknazarian, in addition to many others who have enriched the culture, were Kurds of Ezedi descent.

Beyond the Ezedi influence, the Kurmanji dialect is supported by significant Islamic literature, including the "*Mewlûda Kurmancî*" by Mela Hesen Bateyi (1417-1495), which comprises Kurdish verses

---

* [Video], Êla Redkan ELEGEZ . "Zerê - İlk Kürt Filmi - 1926", 20 Mar 2020.
<https://www.youtube.com/watch?v=cHahi-InKns>

recited on the Prophet Muhammad's birthday. Other notable works include *"Yûsif û Zuleyxa"* (1586) by Salim Salman, a collection of poems by Melayê Cizîrî (1570-1640), *"Mem û Zîn"* by Ahmad Khani (1651-1707), and *"Zembîlfiroş"* by Feqiyê Teyran (1590-1660).

The Botan Emirate (early 8th century to 1847) played a significant role in preserving the status of Kurmanji, particularly under the rule of the last Mîr, Bedirxan Beg, who harbored ambitions for full sovereign independence. Similar support is evident today in Rojava, where Kurmanji has been established as a formal standard for education, media, and administration.

For this dialect to be generalized as a single formal variety and to enhance intelligibility with other dialects, it is necessary to improve its syntax and orthographic representation of phonemes. For instance, adopting a single grapheme for the interchanging phonemes such as Sorani 'W' /ʊ/ versus Kurmanji /v/ would help unify the spelling of words like 'Av' and 'Aw'. This could be achieved by selecting a new grapheme or using 'W' instead of 'V' as it can represent both sounds, similar to the variation of 'W' in English and German.

Digraphia

Formal Kurmanji underwent a diachronic digraphia, sequentially enriched by various orthographic systems: Arabic-Persian, Latin, Cyrillic, Armenian, and Ezedi alphabets. The Arabic-based Persian system was initially used in modern publications, with the first newsletter, "*Kurdistan*," published in Cairo in 1882 by Muqdad Bedirxan (1858-1915). This writing system was common among all dialects and was later adopted by the Kingdom of Kurdistan (1921-1925) as the system of Sorani writing. Until then, this alphabet maintained practical Kurdish orthographic unity. However, the aftermath of World War I, particularly the collapse of the Russian and Ottoman Empires, necessitated linguistic modifications to qualify Kurdish for new tasks.

Following the formation of the Soviet Union in 1917, Kurdish was permitted for use in publication and education for the first time. Initially, the West Armenian alphabet was adopted due to the lack of a dedicated Kurdish writing system. However, for further

IIX. Kurdish Language Strategy

grammatical enhancement, the decision was made to adopt a Latin-based alphabet.

The first Latinization was initiated after an extensive process by Armenian orientalist Joseph Orbeli (1887-1961) and Georgian-born historian and linguist Nikolai Marr (1865-1934). The system was approved by the Soviet Korenization "*коренизация*" committee in 1928 before being finalized by Isahak Marogulov (1868-1933) and Kurdish novelist Arab Shamilov (1897-1978). This alphabet was used continuously until the 1940s for all Kurdish publications, including the Communist Party newsletter "The New Path" (*Rja Təzə*). However, as the system did not live for long, the second Latinization was devised by Kurdish linguist and politician Celadet Alî Bedirxan (1893-1951). Termed "**Kurdmanji**," he introduced the system in his book "*Bingehên Gramera Kurdmancî*" [Basics of Kurdish Grammar], published in 1931. The following year, he implemented his new form in the bi-monthly magazine '*Hawar*', under the authority of French-mandated Syria. The new system became known as the Hawar alphabet.

This modern systemization of grammar and alphabet is regarded as a linguistic revolution and a historical step toward utilizing the language for the nation's interests. Yet, despite the intent to establish a comprehensive Kurdish writing system, both Latinization efforts by Marogulov and Bedirxan, as well as the Persian-based Sorani system developed by Sa'ed Kaban and finalized by Col. Tawfiq Wahbi, were limited to specific dialectal regions. This limitation was not due to a lack of competency but rather the result of hasty efforts, insufficient resources on the subject, and the challenging nature of cross-dialect communication. Bedirxan's term "Kurdmanji" was an endeavor to establish Kurmanji as the sole legitimate formal standard of Kurdish. He wrote:

"*2- The Kurdmanji language: the Kurdmanji language is the language of the Kurdmanji nation in which the Kurdmanji nation speaks, writes, and publicly communicates thoughts.*" (*)

---

* (Bedirxan, 1994, p 15).
"2 - Zimane Kurdmancî : Zimane kurdmancî zimane milete kurdmanc e. Kurdmanc pe daxevin, dinivîsînin û bi gotinen din his û fikren xwe pe eşkere dikin."

The oversight in T. Wahbi's system of ignoring other dialects was not rectified by C. Bedirxan's approach. Instead, Bedirxan essentially replicated the principle but applied it to a different region of speakers. Consequently, both systems require reformation if either is to be selected as the unique formal variety. The geographical expansion necessitates greater phonological tolerance to accommodate phonetic diversity within a comprehensive and inclusive system.

In addition to the Arabic (Persian), Armenian, and Latin scripts, the Cyrillic alphabet was employed in the USSR following the dissolution of "Red Kurdistan" (Курдистанский уезд). The Armenian authorities decided to replace the Latin script with Cyrillic; the Kurdish linguist Prof. Heciyê Cindî (1908-1990) was tasked with this mission in 1941, and the Armenian government adopted the new alphabet in 1946 for Kurdish education and publications. The Cyrillic alphabet was also used in Georgia and Azerbaijan.

Synchronic Digraphia

In addition to the phenomenon of *diachronic digraphia*, there is an emerging *synchronic digraphia* associated with the dialect. Despite the conventional adoption of the Latin script by most prominent Kurmanji figures and institutions, there is a trend towards limited publication in Southern Kurdistan (where Kurmanji, specifically Bahdinani, is spoken) using the Arabic-Sorani alphabet.

A previous instance of synchronic digraphia occurred when Kurmanji was written using the Ezedi alphabet, which was originally utilized for writing the sacred scriptures of the Ezedi religious community. The existence of multiple writing systems contributes to an increase in the number of spelling variants for each word in the language's lexicon. Furthermore, the presence of different grammatical rules across these systems adds complexity to the formal use of the language.

8.2.1.3 Gorani-Zaza (Dimli)

Often referred to as "*Hawrami*" or "*Hawramani*" in Southern Kurdistan, and "Zaza" or "Dimli" in the north. Historically was the literary dialect and lingua franca of the Ardalan vassaldom (1169–

IIX. Kurdish Language Strategy

1867), which ruled Eastern Kurdistan for seven centuries, specifically in the region of modern Kurdistan province Sanandaj. Consequently, it is regarded as the oldest living Kurdish dialect in terms of script and literature. According to Kurdologists, many of the earliest epics and stanzas of Modern Kurdish were composed in Gorani, with some preserved in written form and others transmitted orally through generations. Additionally, it is the dialect of the Yarsani cult's sacred book "*Saranjam*," thus holding significant spiritual prestige among its followers.

A debate exists regarding the origin of this dialect, with some arguing that it is an independent branch of the Iranian languages rather than a Kurdish dialect. Others have suggested it might be a dialect of Modern Persian. However, the speakers of Gorani/Zaza assert their Kurdish identity by referring to their language as "Kurdish" and identifying themselves as "Kurds". This dialect has attracted considerable interest from Western researchers, who have explored its phonetic distinctions and syntactic rules. Some scholars have hesitated to classify it as a Kurdish dialect, which may be due to insufficient data, the limited depth of research, or political motivations—particularly those supported by the Turkish state to deny the Kurdish language's geographical expansion. Additionally, Western linguists often face fieldwork challenges and authoritative obstacles when conducting extended studies among speakers.

In general, as the borderline between a dialect and a full-fledged language is a nuanced and subjective concept, for some linguists, variant phonemes indicate a significant linguistic divergence, while others consider these variations less consequential.

According to the German scholar Terry Lynn Todd, this dialect is a distinct, non-Kurdish language, more closely related to modern Persian than to Kurdish. As part of his Ph.D. project at the University of Michigan, Todd interviewed twenty speakers from Anatolian villages, accompanied by a local guide whose identity remained confidential for security reasons. His research focused on the phonemes, morphemes, syntax, and verb conjugation rules of the dialect. Todd's work, titled "*A Grammar of Dimili, Also Known as Zaza*" was published in 1985, in which he cited Karl Hadank's opinion that the name "Dimili" is a metathesis of "Daylemi," referring to Daylam, an old name for an area on the south coast of the Caspian Sea. (Hadank, 1932, p. 4) Ultimately, Todd (2008, vi) acknowledged the Kurdish identity of the speakers, despite that he maintained that the language itself is distinct from Kurdish:

"*Dimili speakers today consider themselves to be Kurds and resent scholarly conclusions which indicate that their language is not Kurdish. Speakers of Dimili are Kurds psychologically, socially, culturally, economically, and politically.*"

On the other hand, Russian philologist Zare A. Yusupova, a professor at Saint Petersburg State University specializing in the Kurdish language, emphasized that Gorani is one of the Kurdish dialects. In her book, "*The Kurdish Dialect Gorani as Represented in the Literary Monuments from the 18th-19th Centuries*" (1998), she addressed topics such as phonetics, morphology, and syntax, in addition to a glossary of the Gorani lexicon. She analyzed previous publications on Gorani grammar, including the first information provided by British scholar Charles Hieu in 1881, who considered Gorani a variety of Persian. Yusupova refuted his opinion based on insufficient data and also disputed the conclusions of David MacKenzie's work published in 1966. She stated that Hawrami represents one of the southern varieties of the Kurdish language and naturally borders other South Kurdish varieties of Sulaymaniyah, Sanandaj, and Kermanshah (Yusupova, 2017). The major constraint to linguistic development and the failure to maintain a linguistic standard is the dispersal of speakers in isolated remote communities separated by vast geographical distances and international borders. These areas include the eastern part (Pavah), the southern regions (Halabja and the Shabak area in Nineveh), and the northern enclave of Dersim, Bingol, and the surrounding countryside.

Historically, the dialect was the dominant variety used in literature and the judiciary, as well as in the religious texts of the Yarsan cult. Also, it was employed by many poets to create their masterpieces, including Mele Perîşan (1356–1431), Besarani (1641-1702), Khanai Kubadi (1700-1759), Ranjuri (1750-1810), Sayidi (1784-1848), Mawlawi (1806-1882), Wali Diwana (1826–1881), and Komashi (20th century).

The Dutch linguist Michiel Leezenberg (1993, p. 8) wrote:

"*As said, towards the end of the eighteenth century, the Erdelan court was eclipsed by the nearby Baban court centered at*

IIX. Kurdish Language Strategy

Sulaymaniyah, the poets of which had until then mostly written in the prestigious Gorani dialect, but from the early 1800s on wrote in Sorani, which then rose considerably in status. Nowadays, Gorani is a mere shadow of its past: it is largely spoken by impoverished and isolated peasants, and has practically become extinct as a literary dialect; for as far as I know, only one poet, Sayyid Tahir Hashemi, has written Gorani poetry in recent years; his Diwan was published in Mahabad shortly after his death"

However, as an old and isolated variety, its limited lexicon may require borrowing words from other more vibrant dialects, where loan words may enhance intelligibility with the remaining varieties.

8.2.1.4 Southern (Pahlawani), Luri, Faili

Southern dialect, linguistically known as "Southern Kurmanji", "Luri" in Iran, "Faili" in Iraq, or "Pahlawani", is a large continuum of sub-dialects and is deemed a bridge that historically connects Kurdish and the mother language (the ancient Pahlavi) and geographically with the sister modern Persian. Many researchers, including Dr. Ismail Qamandar, reject the endonym 'Luri' and the exonym 'Faili', preferring the term *Southern dialect(s)*. Morphologically, a significant proportion of the morphemes share the same origin with the other Kurdish dialects and Persian, in a varying degree of phonetic bias.

Traditionally, there has been little inclination to develop an independent writing system for this dialect, likely due to its geographical proximity to Sorani and Persian, both of which are formally written and exhibit considerable mutual intelligibility. As a result, the Southern dialect has remained largely colloquial, permeated by loan words from standard Persian in Iran and Arabic in Iraq.

The only group of speakers that tends to borrow words from other Kurdish dialects is found in the Khanaqin region. However, in response to the contemporary need for a dedicated writing system, particularly due to the accelerating expansion of media usage, efforts have been made to standardize the grammar and vocabulary of the Southern dialect. The most notable self-initiated effort is attributed to Dr. Qamandar, who developed a system based on the Latin alphabet, aiming to approximate Kurmanji while simultaneously standardizing the dialect by emphasizing syntactical similarities with Sorani, which served as the primary source of loan words. He stated *(*)*:

"*5. I took the rules of Sorani as a basis for my proposals, due to the uncountable closeness facets of the two dialects. As for the dictation in the second section, the Kurmanji dialect was taken as a basis.*"

Qamandar's writing system integrates distinctive phonemes into the Kurmanji alphabet, addressing specific phonetic features such as the diphthong that combines the vowels /ɪ/ and /ʊ/ to produce a long vowel /ɪʊ/, akin to the Turkish 'Ü' as in "Bütün" Eng. 'all'. This phoneme, represented by the grapheme 'Ü,' appears in some Southern accents, in words such as "Düêt" Eng. 'daughter', and "Bü" Eng. became. He preserves the dialectal syntactical rules as unique grammatical characteristics, nonetheless, the most notable difference from Sorani is in the transitive past tense. Unlike the English syntax order (Subject-Verb-Object), Sorani's syntax is (Object-Subject-Verb) while Southern's is (Subject-Object-Verb). Additionally, while the subject pronoun is separate in English (e.g., "I"), it is attached as "M" in both Kurdish dialects but suffixed to the subject in Sorani and to the verb in the Southern dialect. The following table demonstrates the syntax order differences.

Language	*Sentence*	*Pronoun*	*Syntax*
English	*I* saw Alan	Deattached	SVO
Kurmanji	*Min* Alan dît	Deattached	SOV
Sorani	Alan*M* bini ئالان‌م بینی	Sbject suffix	OSV
Southern	~~*Min*~~ Alan dî*M* من ئالان دیم	Verb suffix	SOV
Pahlavi	Az (Man) Alan dîd-*im*	Verb suffix	SOV

The distinctive syntax order (OSV) in Sorani is uncommon among dialects, including the root language Pahlavi. This divergent approach can lead to misunderstandings where the subject is perceived as the object in other dialects and vice versa, effectively reversing the

---

* (Qamandar, 2014, p. 65).

"٥. اتخذت قواعد اللهجة السورانية كأساس لمقترحي هذا، لقرابة اللهجتين ولأوجه التشابه الكثيرة بينهما والتي لا تعد لاتحصى. أما الاملاء في القسم الثاني أتخذت املاء اللهجة الكورمانجية كأساس".

IIX. Kurdish Language Strategy

meaning of a sentence. For instance, the Sorani sentence "Alanam bini" (I saw Alan) would be interpreted as "Alan saw me" in the Southern dialect. In this context, the Southern SOV is closest to the mother language Pahlavi, suggesting that the syntactical deviation occurred in Sorani, not in other dialects. Regarding the relationship between Southern Kurdish and Pahlavi, some linguists and historians assert that the contemporary form of dialect retains significant similarities with ancient roots. Iranian linguist Aliriza Asadi (2017, pp. 64-65, 106) confirms the heritage of both the Parthian and Sassanid versions of Pahlavi in the current Southern Kurdish dialect:

"Language in Ilam retains a strong link with ancient Iranic languages (the Parthian and the Sassanid Pahlavi). By comparing the recent Kurdish Malikshahi vocabulary with the ancient Iranic language, a conclusion may be reached that the majority of the words are either of Pahlavi or rootable. That is in addition to the phonology, structural and socioreligious concepts, nouns, and basic and vernacular expressions".

Asadi's reference to the colloquial form of *Malikshahi*, the Kurdish tribe that dwells in Ilam province, was not intended to excogitate the tribal vernacular, but merely a random attempt to exemplify the linguistic status in the Pahlawani landscape. Phonologically, the dialect retains the original Pahlavi phonemes, such as 'M', similar to the Gorani sub-dialects. In contrast, this phoneme shifts in both Sorani (to 'W' /ʊ/) and Kurmanji (to 'V') when it appears at the end of a word or between vowels. Here is an example to compare the shift occurs to the phoneme /m/:

English	*Pahlavi*	*Southern*	*Gorani*	*Sorani*	*Kurmanji*
Name	Nām	Nam نام	Nam	Naw ناو	Nav
Prayer	Namāz	Namaz نماز	Nimêz	Nwej نوێژ	Nivêj
Half	Nēm	Nim نیم	Nim	New نیو	Nîv
Raw	Xām	Xam خام	Xam	Xaw خاو	Xav
Land	Zamig	Zamin زمین	Zemîn	Zewi زەوی	Zevî
Co- Such in Compatriot	Ham	Ham هم همولاتي Hamwelati	Ham Hamwelati	Haw هاو هاولاتي Hawwelati	Hev Hevwelatî

Many poets have composed their works in this dialect, including the oldest known Kurdish poet, *Baba Tahir Hamadani*, who lived in the eleventh century, producing philosophical quatrains that are still recited in modern Iran. Baba Tahir's poetic style is known as *Pahlaviat*, named after the region of *Pahla* to be distinguished from the royal court language *Dari* دري. Pahla پهله (the ancient Media Empire), according to the Ruzbih pur Daduya known as Ibn al-Muqaffa ابن المقفع (Died 759 AD), encompassed five districts (Nahavand, Azerbaijan, Hamadan, Ray, and Isfahan).

The other well-known poet was Mele Perîşan (1356–1431). He was born into a family of the Qiaswand tribe in the ancient town of Dinavar, located in what is now the Kermanshah province. (*) Perîşan used the Laki sub-dialect for his works, in addition to the Gorani dialect, as seen in his religious diwan "*Perîşan-nama.*" An example of Laki's vocabulary is evident in his poem:

Saqi bawerî jami pî mesti	ساقی باوری جامی پی مستی
Sudem mestîen zianem jî hesti	سودم مستین زیانم ژه هستی
Fedat bem saqi ter zuwanem ke	فدات بم ساقی ترزوانم که
Man darddaram dawi giyanem ke	من درددارم داوی گیانم که

"May you, barmaid, pass a glass.
Only when drunk I do gain, losing when staid.
Kindly moisten my brittle tongue.
Though healing away my spirit's pain."

Observe the distinctive Southern words: in the first line, "Bawerî" literally means 'Bring' (to me) equivalent to the Sorani بهێنن 'Bihînin' and Kurmanji 'bîne', not to be confused with the verb "Were" وەرە (Come) in Sorani and Kurmanji. It closely resembles the Persian cognate "Biawer" بیاور. Additionally, in the third line, the uncommon open compound word "Terzuwan" ترزوان Eng. 'wet tongue' is used.

---

* Iraj Kazimi, Iraj. Kayan Farhangi. Issue 109. May 1994, p 40-41
کاظمی، ایرج. کیهان فرهنگی. اردیبهشت 1373. شماره 109؟ ص 40-41
<https://www.noormags.ir/view/fa/articlepage/16944/-قلمرو-در-عرفان
ملا<2=rownumber&337.41843=score&ملا20%پریشان=q?مشاهیر-ادب-لر

IIX. Kurdish Language Strategy

This term comprises the adjective "Ter" تەڕ Eng. 'wet', preceding the object "Zuwan" زوان Eng. 'Tongue'. The precedence of the adjective is a Pahlavi form that is still used in Pashto, the adjective and object order in compound words in Persian, however, this order is nearly abandoned in modern Kurdish dialects. Furthermore, the syncopic word "Ke," employed as an end rhyme in the third and fourth lines, replaces the imperative verb "Bika" بیکە Eng. 'do', with the open syllable "Bi" removed.

8.2.1.5 Arguments

For the sake of saving time and effort, selecting an existing formal standard is a defensible option. This approach was effective in the unification of German, Italian, and Spanish. However, These examples occurred in previous centuries as direct consequences of wars or the dominance of certain dialects over others. Therefore, this option may not align with contemporary circumstances. In modern times, there are potential drawbacks to preferring one dialect over the others, such as anticipated resistance from speakers of the marginalized dialects and the possibility of long-running debates with opponents.

8.2.2 Coining a New Standard

Establishing a linguistic standard is an academic endeavor achievable by linguists and scholars through comprehensive applied research encompassing all current and future aspects of social, political, and economic structures. Since this initiative is not an official resolution nor dependent on authorization, the project of creating a new standard for formal language can commence at any time, with the role of authority becoming pertinent at a subsequent stage.

However, for a new standard to serve as a comprehensive linguistic framework, its lexicon should consider drawing from the original morphemes, rather than relying on recent pronunciation. As morphemes are continually modified in different regions, modern pronunciations diverge, resulting in dialectal discrepancies.

The existing Kurdish formal standards were developed with shallow orthography, prioritizing the phonological structure of local vernaculars at the expense of cross-dialectal specifics and the origin of the morphemes. At the beginning of the 20th century, the tight deadlines and cumbersome communication methods made it difficult for Isahak Marogulov (Soviet Armenia, 1928), Col. Tawfiq Wahbi (Iraq, 1930), and Mir Celadet Bedirxan (Syria, 1931) to consider philology and historical linguistics adequately.

To date, the lack of a broad, innovative vision and the neglect of diachronic phonemic shifts have resulted in fragmented orthography. The technical limitations had hindered Marogulov from fully comprehending Sorani or conducting field research in the geographically closer Zaza region. Similarly, Bedirxan and Wahbi neglected other dialects and previous orthographies. However, given the advanced facilities currently available, the extensive knowledge of linguistics, and the flexible schedule, the potential to establish modern, robust, and unifying language standards is now within reach.

Linguistic integrity necessitates a thorough consideration of Gorani (Zaza) and Southern (Pahlawani) dialects in the establishment of formal language standards. Effective unification may not be achieved by merely combining Kurmanji and Sorani. Without a critical step to practically incorporate other dialects, any attempt at unification or modernization will confront further challenges.

In addition to lexical differences, grammatical variations further distinguish these dialects from one another. Linguists engaged in developing a new formal dialect recognize that vernacular grammar evolves based on the natural use of speakers, not rigid rules. This often introduces a margin of error in the interpretation of complex ideas. Thus, the formal variety must aim for semantic precision with necessary grammatical amendments for greater accuracy. The challenge lies in determining how far the formal variety can push the rules to achieve the highest precision while ensuring sentences remain intelligible to vernacular speakers.

For instance, the present tense prefixes "de" ده and "ee" ئە are used interchangeably without semantic distinction, and at the same time, there is no future tense in Sorani grammar. It would have been practical to differentiate tenses by assigning each prefix to a specific tense when modern Sorani grammar was first introduced. Bedirxan,

IIX. Kurdish Language Strategy

however, designated 'di' as a prefix for the present tense and "e" as a separable prefix for the future tense. Inspired by Bedirxan, more advanced grammatical rules can be formulated to enhance accuracy.

8.2.2.1 Koiné language

To facilitate communication, mixed communities of different linguistic backgrounds sharing a certain urban landscape tend to simplify grammatical rules and generalize vocabulary. This linguistic fusion can result in **pidginization** or **creolization**. Pidginization occurs when speakers of unintelligible languages develop a mixed variety, defined as a *pidgin language*, for limited usage as a common means of communication. Creolization, however, follows when speakers of a pidgin language adopt it as their native language, replacing their original varieties.

Rapidly developing cities such as Arbil, Diyarbakir, and Kermanshah, which attract a diverse workforce from various regions, are becoming linguistic hubs of many co-existing mutually intelligible varieties. This dialectal leveling led to the emergence of a new dialect, described as "Koiné," a term derived from the ancient Greek common dialect that became the lingua franca during the Hellenistic and Roman eras. Koineization arises to meet the community's needs in markets, schools, and social settings, eventually becoming the city's distinguished variety over several generations. In contemporary times, with the accelerating expansion of mass media and the widespread availability of easy-to-use communication tools. A Koiné may extend beyond city borders to become a regionally adapted variety.

Despite forceful Arabization, Turkification, and, to some extent, Persification policies, the Kurdish language has maintained deep roots in social life. Consequently, no pidgin or creole languages have emerged from Kurdish and neighboring languages. However, the widespread use of modern communication facilities such as television and internet services is driving a slow national-level process of koineization. As koine dialects gain prominence, marginalizing other dialects, it is expected to accelerate and facilitate the natural process of linguistic unification.

8.2.2.2 Rule of No Rules

No Kurdish dialect has adhered to preset rules, neither in its evolution nor development over the past centuries, whether in grammar or vocabulary. It is more accurate to state that neither Kurdish nor other vernacular languages inherently possess rules. Colloquial languages evolve through habitual practices among speaker populations, and only later are rules established by linguists to create a formalized structure for accurate communication.

The primary issue in formalizing a vernacular language is managing the balance between the spoken "convention-based" forms and the formal "rule-based" forms. This management involves determining how closely rules should adhere to spoken language, potentially sacrificing natural speaking habits for the sake of accuracy and mutual intelligibility. Linguists, when formulating these rules, aim not to strictly follow phonological habits or morphological traditions but to create guidelines that may not necessarily align with any specific variety, even if it is predominant.

For example, the revived Hebrew lexicon was initially created by the Russian lexicographer Eliezer Ben-Yehuda using approximately 8000 Biblical Hebrew root words to replace various languages spoken by the Jewish diaspora, such as Yiddish and Ladino. His work faced rejection, and his family was ostracized by the Orthodox Jewish community for what they considered the sacrilegious use of the language they believed should be reserved for sacred texts. The first native speaker of modern Hebrew was Ben-Yehuda's son, Ben-Zion Ben-Yehuda (1882-1943), later renamed Itamar Ben-Avi. Despite initial resistance, the language gained recognition as official in Palestine in 1922 under the British mandate.

In comparison, the simultaneous Kurdish Latinization effort by the Soviet linguist Isahak Marogulov, despite focusing on the phonological structure of a small community of speakers, could have become the standard Kurdish orthography if supported by a Kurdish state or endorsed by scholars and activists. His work was ignored by Taufiq Wahbi, and Wahbi's work was subsequently neglected by Celadet Bedirxan. In the absence of state enforcement, Marogulov, Wahbi, and Bedirxan attempted to accommodate a wide range of dialects but were constrained by local colloquial limitations and

IIX. Kurdish Language Strategy

phonetic details. Moreover, Wahbi and Heciyê Cindî exaggerated the importance of phonology by prioritizing linguistic transparency, resulting in a local phonemic language with a shallow orthography. The diacritics they added were ineffective semantically, as the Arabic-Persian writing system, with its flexibility in containing vowel phonemes, offered better pronunciation options for speakers.

These efforts failed to establish a common, national-level standard as a unified formal variety required to be liberated from the influences of locality and the constraints of colloquial phonology.

8.3.3 Pahlavi Based

The Pahlavi language, serving as the morphological reservoir of the Kurdish lexicon, provides the root cognates of contemporary words and offers a rich resource for affixes. Additionally, examining the dialectal phonetic variations of synonymous lexemes is crucial for selecting the most suitable cognates for a unified dictionary.

As the progenitor of several Iranic languages, including Kurdish, Baluchi, and Pashto, Pahlavi can assist these languages in distinguishing loanwords from anciently inherited morphemes, thereby enhancing their capacity for inflection and derivation.

8.3.3.1 Resource for Affixes

As an agglutinative, similar to the majority of Indo-European languages, the expansion of Kurdish vocabulary primarily relies on affixes. The prefixes and suffixes that have been lost over the past centuries can be retrieved from Pahlavi, which not only utilizes pronoun suffixes (Blochet, p. 60) but is also sufficiently rich for Kurdish to achieve greater flexibility. This is particularly important for generating modern terms in fields such as science, economics, social affairs, and commodity products. For instance, the suffix "-war," as seen in "Umed**war**im" /ʊmɪədəwˈaːrɪm/, Eng. 'I hope', (rendered in Pahlavi "Book" script as "ܗܐܝܟܘܪ", corresponding to the sequence: ⟨a⟩ '܁', ⟨m⟩ '܁', ⟨j⟩ '܁', ⟨d⟩ '܁', ⟨u⟩ 'l', ⟨a⟩ '܁', ⟨r⟩

'ۏ', and ⟨m⟩ 'م') still exists in the Sorani dictionary as ئومێدوارم. This word aggregates the following morphemes:

1. Omid /ʊːmæd/, /ʊmˈjd/ ئومێد (ســێـ) Eng. *Hope*: the stem was phonetically biased by the regular dropping of the phonemes /m/ and /d/, to Sor. "Heewa" هیوا, and Kurm. hêvî.
2. War /ˈwɑr/ وار (ــوار): a suffix used for emphasizing the stem's sememe as an intense analogous. Similar to the English "-*ful*", e.g. in "hopeful", it gives the meaning of "full of", "having the quality of", and "tending to". (*)
3. Im /ɪm/ م (ـم): the speaker's singular possessive adverb suffix. It also serves as the first-person singular pronoun.

In general, modern Kurdish already employs several suffixes inherited from its parent language, Pahlavi, such as::

- "-dar" (*Kurm*. -dar, *Sor*. ـدار -, *Eng*. With):
    - *Kurm*. Rê**dar**, *Sor*. ڕێزدار, *Eng*. Respectful.
    - *Kurm*. Dil**dar**, *Sor*. دڵدار, *Eng*. Lover, Happy, a person who shows condolences.
    - *Kurm*. Hêvî**dar**, *Sor*. هیوادار, *Eng*. Hopeful.

- "-stan" (*Kurm*. -istan, *Sor*. ـستان -, *Eng*. Land, distinguished place or time):
    - *Kurm*. Kurdi**stan**, *Sor*. کوردستان, *Eng*. Kurdistan).
    - *Kurm*. Zivi**stan**, *Sor*. زستان, *Eng*. Winter.
    - *Kurm*. Dibi**stan**, *Sor*. دبستان, *Eng*. Primary school.

- "-an" (*Kurm*. -an, *Sor*. ان -, *Eng*. Plural marker):
    - *Kurm*. Jin**an** /ʒɪnˈan/ , *Sor*. ژنان, *Eng*. Women.
    - *Kurm*. Dar**an**, *Sor*. داران, *Eng*. Trees.
    - *Kurm*. Xwendekar**an**, *Sor*. خوێندکاران, *Eng*. Students.

Also inherited several prefixes like:

---

* https://www.oxfordlearnersdictionaries.com/definition/english/ful

IIX. Kurdish Language Strategy

- "bê-" (*Kurm.* Bê, *Sor.* -ﺑێ, *Eng.* Without):
  - *Kurm.* **Bê**kar, *Sor.* بێکار, *Eng.* Unemployed.
- "ne-" (*Kurm.* , *Sor* - نە, *Eng.* The negation marker):
  - *Kurm.* **Ne**xweş, *Sor.* نەخۆش, *Eng.* Not well, ill.
- "ser-" (*Kurm.* Ser-, *Sor.* -سەر, *Eng.* Top, head of a group):
  - *Kurm.* **Ser**nivîskar, *Sor.* سەرنووسەر, *Eng.* Editor-in-Chief.

Modern Kurdish, like other agglutinative languages, is capable of incorporating additional prefixes and suffixes that enhance terminology across various fields. Utilizing the abundance of original affixes provides essential resources, reduces dependency on foreign loanwords, and consequently strengthens the language's structure. This enhancement grants its speakers greater confidence in the competitive landscape of regional language ideologies.

8.3.3.2 Writing system

The orthographic systems used for Kurmanji and Sorani have not yet conceptualized modern Kurdish as a fully integrated language. Arabic-Persian, Latin, Cyrillic, and even modern Sorani scripts do not consistently represent its phonological structure and have only created transparent systems for certain local dialects. This lack of a comprehensive approach has failed to address simple issues, leading to complex consequences such as the interchangeable pronunciation like the phonemes 'V' and 'W' or the absence of the 'Kh' /ɣ/ خ phoneme in Gorani.

The Pahlavi "Book" system, however, offers a practical solution for the first issue by representing both phonemes 'W' and 'V' with a single grapheme, 'l'. This letter accommodates both forms of pronunciation, as exemplified by the Kurmanji and Sorani cognates "Av" /ˈav/ and "Aw" /ˈaʊ/ ناو *Eng.* Water, which can be written as 'ﺳﺎﻟ' and read as 'Aw' or 'Av' depending on the accent in use. This flexibility allows both dialects to choose their preferred pronunciation without disrupting the unity of the Kurdish lexicon.

Historically, Pahlavi was associated with multiple writing systems, evolving from cuneiform to Parthian, and eventually to the Sasanian "Book" script. (MacKenzie, 1971, p. xi) The following figure shows the letters of the Book script.

' ('ālep̄)*	ᴊᴅ	l (lāmed̠)	ᴌ
b (bēṭ)	ᴊ	m (mēm)	ᴓ
g (gimel)	ᴅ	s (sāmek̠)	ᴓ
h (hē)	ᴨ	p (pē)	ᴓ
w (wāw)	ᴉ	ś/š (ś/šīn)	ᴓ
z (zayin)	ᴊ	t (tāw)	ᴘ
k (kap̄)	ᴊ		

The following example demonstrates the spelling using the *Book* script by listing this sample:

Pahlavi	Latin	Sorani
ᴉ	V	ڤ
ᴉ	W	و
ᴊ	A	ا
ᴊ	Ş	ش
ᴋ	N	ن

The pronunciation of words such as 'Av', 'Şev', 'Nav', and 'Van' can be standardized along with their synonyms 'Aw', 'Şew', 'Naw', and 'Wan' within a unified spelling system. This issue has already been addressed in the right-to-left script 'Book':

✓ 'ᴊᴉ': made of the two letters 'ᴊ' (A) and 'ᴉ' (W and V), can be read as "Av" and "Aw" ناو (Eng. 'Water') at the same time.

✓ 'ᴊᴉ': made of 'ᴊ' (Sh) and 'ᴉ', read as "Şev" /ʃəv'/ and "Şew" /ʃəu'/ شەو (Eng. 'Night').

✓ 'ᴋᴊᴉ ': made of 'ᴋ' ('N'), 'ᴊ' ('A'), and 'ᴉ', read as 'Nav' /naːv/ and 'Naw' /naː ʊ/ (Eng. 'Name').

✓ 'ᴉᴊᴋ': made of 'ᴉ' ('W' or 'V'), 'ᴊ' ('A'), and 'ᴋ' ('N'), read as Van and Wan.

IIX. Kurdish Language Strategy

By omitting short vowels, and representing them as insignificant diacritics, the Pahlavi script may allow for a degree of tolerance in accommodating phonetic variations across different dialects. This feature is similar to modern Arabic and Hebrew and makes the Pahlavi script particularly suitable for Kurdish, as it comprises many dialects of low mutual intelligibility. Consequently, the Pahlavi writing system, with minor modifications becomes more applicable to Kurdish than the Arabic or Latin-based alphabets.

Compared to Kurdish, most nations within the region have preserved their ancient writing systems, successfully maintaining linguistic unity. For example, Hebrew, Armenian, Georgian, Hindi, Russian, Greek, Syriac, and Arabic have remained loyal to their inherited orthographies. In contrast, the Pahlavi script was abandoned and neglected for centuries. Only Turkish, for a historical lack of a proper writing system, and Pahlavi descendant languages, influenced mainly by religious beliefs, have adapted to the Arabic-Persian and later to the Latin alphabet. However, appropriate modifications are essential to adapt the system to contemporary needs. This renovation would involve increasing the number of letters, modifying letterforms and ligatures, and creating relevant typefaces. With adequate support, the revitalized Pahlavi script could flourish and become a distinctive sociolinguistic symbol of the Kurdish nation, similar to the symbolic status of Arabic letters among Arab nations.

8.3.3.3 Old Scripts

Many scripts have been used over the centuries, ranging from the ancient Old Iranic, also known as Old Persian, which was primarily used before Pahlavi, to contemporary Kurdish. The texts of Old Iranic were written in cuneiform scripts, as exemplified by the Behistun Inscription. This significant relief (22 x 7.8 meters), located on a cliff at Mount Behistun, 30 kilometers east of Kermanshah in Eastern Kurdistan, contains 414 lines of Old Iranic text in five columns. Eventually, cuneiform was replaced by the Pahlavi writing system.

Additionally, an unnamed ancient script was mentioned by Ibn Waḥshiyya, the Nabataean toxicologist who died in 930 CE. According to his accounts, this rare script was used for Kurdish:

> *"Another ancient script contains some obsolete letters, which Kurds allegedly claim was used by Pinoshad and in which Moses wrote the Torah. Additionally, both figures purportedly employed this script to document all their knowledge and arts."* (*)

In his book شوق المستهام في معرفة رموز الأقلام [Epistemophile Longing to Lore Pen Codes], Ibn Waḥshiyya added:

> *"I have seen about thirty books of this script in Baghdad, in addition to other two I had have in the Levante, one on viticulture and palm cultivation, and the other deals with irrigation and methods of extracting water in the unclaimed lands, though, I have translated them from Kurdish to Arabic for the benefit of the public."* (†)

Below is his illustration of the script.

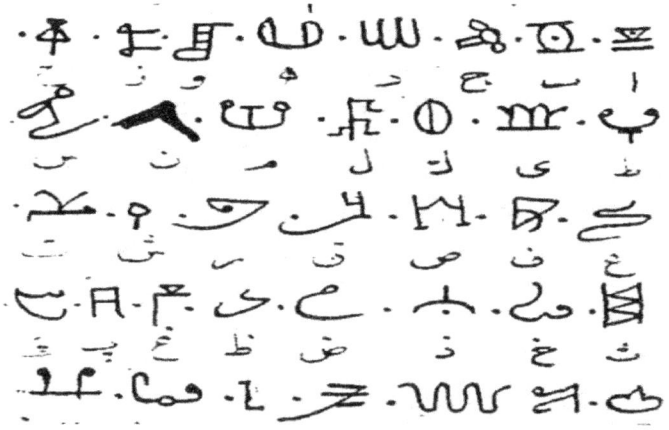

---

* Ibn Waḥshiyya (n.d/2004). part 8, p204
"صفة قلم اخر من الاقلام القديمة وفيه حروف زايدة عن القواعد الحرفية تدعي الاكراد وتزعم انه القلم الذي كتب به بينوشاد وماسي التوراتي جميع علومهما وفنونهما وكتبهما بهذا القلم"

† Same source.
"وقد رأيت في بغداد في ناووس من هذا الخط نحو ثلاثين كتاباً وكان عندي منها في الشام كتابين كتاب في افلاح الكرم والنخل وكتاب في علل المياه وكيفية استخراجها واستنباطها من الاراضي المجهولة الاصل فترجمتها من لسان الاكراد الى اللسان العربي لينتفع به ابناء البشر"

IIX. Kurdish Language Strategy

Additionally, the liturgical Ezidi script, attributed to an unknown author, was utilized for two sacred manuscripts, 'Meṣḥefa Reş' and 'Kitêba Cilwe', first published by the Lebanese Christian priest Anastase Marie Al-Karmali in 1911. While the Ezadi community's social organizational structure acknowledges the alphabet, the authenticity of these two manuscripts remains a subject of contention.

8.3.4 Coexistence of Dialects

While a couple of standardized dialects may coexist and are even proven as parallel officials, adopting multiple dialects for formal communication requires the speaking community to achieve fluency in all recognized dialects simultaneously. For instance, the concurrent use of Sorani and Kurmanji in official correspondence, education, and mass media necessitates that individuals attain equal fluency in both dialects to maintain consistency and accuracy in administrative communication.

Global examples of formally adopting multiple varieties include Norway's bidialectalism, Afghanistan's bilingualism, and Turkey's diachronic linguistic variation.

8.3.4.1 Coexistence of Norwegian Dialects

For the past 200 years, dual formal dialects have been employed for official purposes in Norway (see Section 10.2.2), with Bokmål and Nynorsk used simultaneously. However, these dialects do not divide the country into linguistic zones nor are they associated with specific sub-ethnic groups; instead, both are considered national forms of writing. In contrast to Kurmanji and Sorani, which are linked to specific geographic populations, the Norwegian dialects were developed as nationwide varieties, unrelated to specific regions.

Consequently, every Norwegian speaker is equally fluent in both dialects and neither dialect is associated with a particular group of speakers or geographic zone, nor considered a sub-ethnic variety. The concurrent use of both formal writing dialects does not risk national unity for the following reasons:

1. They do not trigger sensitive rivalry among major spoken dialects, thereby preserving a sense of unity.

2. They do not encourage smaller sub-ethnic groups to promote their own dialects as replacements for the national language, avoiding the creation of formal rules and standards that could lead to further linguistic division or disrupt national harmony.

3. They do not stimulate sub-racial sentiments by emphasizing socio-geographical contrasts.

8.3.4.2 Bilingualism in Afghanistan

Although Persian, known as Dari, is spoken by 78% of Afghanistan's multilingual population, (*) the constitution designates two languages for formal use:

> "*Pashto and Dari shall be the official languages of the state. In areas where the majority of the people speak any one of Uzbeki, Turkmani, Pachaie, Nuristani, Baluchi, or Pamiri languages, any of the aforementioned languages, in addition to Pashto and Dari, shall be the third official language, the usage of which shall be regulated by law.*" (†)

Official recognition of multilingualism and the freedom to use local languages and varieties for informal communication have positive effects on social structure.

However, bilingualism in formal communication has not proved to be a practical solution, and thus Dari remains the lingua franca in administrative contexts.

For instance, the Ministry of Education has been unable to implement a bilingual education system where in schools of Kabul, Pashto-speaking students were segregated from their Dari-speaking

---

* https://www.cia.gov/the-world-factbook/countries/afghanistan/

† The Constitution of the Islamic Republic of Afghanistan, 2004, Article 16.

IIX. Kurdish Language Strategy

peers, resulting in education being provided in only one language, that is either Dari or Pashto. (*)

The strategy of class segregation does not meet the definition of bilingual education and has raised concerns about potential negative consequences not only on the system of education, and the sociocultural advancement but also on the national unity.

8.3.4.3 Diachronic Variation of Turkish

Prior to the establishment of the Turkish Republic in 1923, the language of West Anatolian Turkish was spoken in a colloquial form known as Kaba, while the formal was Ottoman. The colloquial language had closer ties to the Turkic tribes' tongues, whereas the Ottoman lexicon was primarily composed of loanwords from Persian and Arabic. This divergence created a linguistic divide where the elite used the Ottoman for formal communication, rendering it unintelligible to ordinary people, particularly those from lower and less educated classes.

The evolution of the current formal dialect began during the era of Turkey's first president, Mustafa Kemal Atatürk. The modernization efforts commenced with the replacement of the Arabic script with the Roman alphabet, crafted by the Armenian linguist Hakob Martayan (who was Turkified to Agop Dilâçar) in 1928 (Russell A., 2019). This initial step was followed by a purification campaign led by the Türk Dil Kurumu (Turkish Language Association), founded in 1932, aiming to eliminate borrowed words, mainly from Arabic and Persian, and replace them with new equivalents rooted in Turkish. This process significantly widened the gap between the two formal dialects (Ottoman and modern Turkish) to the extent that some of Atatürk's speeches became less comprehensible to subsequent generations without translation subtitles.

---

* Abdul Hamid Hatsaandh, The Need For Bilingual Education In Afghanistan – OpEd, April 23, 2019 <https://www.eurasiareview.com/23042019-the-need-for-bilingual-education-in-afghanistan-analysis/>

However, this dual formality did not confuse the administrative system, endanger the unity of the Turkish language, or trigger ethnic divisions. Consistency persisted as the two dialects did not overlap; rather, there was always a single formal set of standards in use at any given time.

IX. Diglossia & Digraphia

"Unity to be real must stand the severest strain without breaking."

Mahatma Gandhi

Diglossia refers to the coexistence of multiple varieties within a single community, each serving different functions: typically, a colloquial spoken form for day-to-day communication and a formal written for official, public announcements, and curriculum use (see Section 7.1.1). Languages such as Arabic, Italian, and Chinese are intensively diglossic, whereas Turkish, English, and Russian exhibit less distinction between standard and spoken dialects and are thus not considered diglossic.

Kurdish is also, in a sense, not diglossic as the differences between standard and nonstandard in each of the forms, Sorani and Kurmanji, are minimal, at the same time it is not monoglossic due to its numerous low-intelligibility dialects, which necessitate the use of multiple varieties for cross-regional communication, and for lacking a common high variety to serve as a diglossic cross-dialectal standard. As a result, determining whether to classify Kurdish as diglossic or as a collection of monoglossic varieties ultimately depends on the perspective of the linguist.

The unity of a language is not indicated by the proximity of spoken dialects but rather by the adoption of a single formal model— represented by a single dialect as a common high (H) form—

regardless of the multitude of spoken varieties and their degree of mutual intelligibility. For a linguistically diverse language, ensuring unity involves finding a comprehensive framework that preserves the multiplicity of spoken dialects while bridging differences through a common intelligible orthographic system. However, the creation of a synthesized variety would inevitably maintain a certain distance from all spoken dialects, similar to formal Arabic, thereby introducing a degree of diglossia.

9.1 Diglossia

Due to the lack of orthographic development over the last millennium, Kurdish has not evolved a linguistic standard to protect lexical entries. Consequently, words have been subject to local biases in sound and definition. The absence of a unified writing system has led to continuous divergence and branching of dialects, impeding the emergence of a high variety. Additionally, in the first half of the twentieth century, the independently developed writing systems for Sorani and Kurmanji, due to their disharmony, further reduced mutual intelligibility.

The establishment of a unified formal dialect as a linguistic umbrella would provide the language with the flexibility to adapt to modern developments without necessitating adjustments to vernaculars or favoring one dialect over another. However, implementing a standard umbrella would inevitably introduce a degree of diglossia, which should be tolerated as a practical solution and adopted in the unique orthographic system. A successful example of diglossia can be seen in the role of classical Arabic, which serves as a universal bridge for all Arabic-speaking communities. Classical Arabic has the potential to evolve and keep pace with sociocultural developments without imposing extra burdens on ordinary speakers. It also enhances intelligibility among various Arabic dialects by providing a well-prepared source of loanwords.

IX. Diglossia & Digraphia

Any effort to establish grammatical and orthographic rules in Kurdish would practically stretch the linguistic diversity between formal and informal communication, creating a degree of diglossia. Given the rich variety of low intelligible vernaculars in Kurdish, similar to Arabic, diglossia is unavoidable if there is a separation between academic and informal communication in a unified Kurdish language.

9.1.1 Bilingualism

Compared to Arabic, the absence of a single unified high variety has fostered bilingualism among Kurdish monoglossic varieties. For better understanding, different groups with low mutual intelligibility tend to use another commonly spoken language (Turkish, Persian, or Arabic). This phenomenon, along with the low fluency in the mother tongue, explains the rising trend of bilingualism among Kurdish speakers. For example, a Kurd from the remote enclave in Khorasan (northeastern Iran) may prefer Persian as a medium of communication in other Kurdish regions. Similarly, a Kurd from Khanaqin might resort to Arabic for fluent exchanges with a Kurd from Afrin. This preference for bilingualism and alternative communication mediums has several long-term implications:

1. It hinders the expansion of Kurdish vocabulary by providing an alternative source for modern terms such as scientific phrases, social expressions, and names of industrial products.

2. The distribution of vocabulary from disparate sources into different dialects—that is, word borrowing from Persian in one region, from Turkish in another, and from Arabic in a third—reduces linguistic harmony and cohesion, and widens the gap in intelligibility over generations.

3. It devalues Kurdish, resulting in a decline in its status to a substratum.

4. The influence of different languages in separated regions further distances these regions. For instance, Kurdish spoken in Turkey causes grammatical shifts and develops a different vocabulary from that spoken in Iran.

5. The prevalence of foreign patterns in day-to-day conversations implies a gradual change in social norms, values, and beliefs.
6. The further isolation of Kurdish speakers by current international borders erodes national sentiment in favor of localized patriotic sentiment.

The Middle East is witnessing intense linguistic competition in which Kurdish lacks the necessary means to compete. Furthermore, its latent capabilities have not been optimally exploited. In contrast, other languages receive substantial support from both intellectuals and authorities, implement well-designed plans, and enjoy a superstratum, granting them a far superior status over Kurdish, especially in multicultural districts. Compared to the low-status Kurdish, Arabic is sacred and enjoys prestige that extends beyond its borders. Turkish holds moral sanctity among all populations of Turkic origin, and Persian, as the language of literature, is characterized by the richness of an enormous heritage accumulated throughout its history. These languages have engaged in sociocultural activities far more extensively than Kurdish, incentivizing large groups of Kurdish speakers to use second languages in which they are equally fluent.

The lack of a solid unified high variety may suppress the natural course of development, relegating Kurdish to a lower substratum and diminishing its social influence among speakers. For example, audiences of sports events, breaking news, and television dramas often turn to other languages for more adequate coverage. In light of the ban on teaching Kurdish in countries such as Turkey and Iran, as well as among Kurdish communities in Iraq and Syria (outside the Kurdish-controlled regions), Kurdish is gradually losing the advantage of being the first choice for its speakers.

9.1.2 Diglossic Tolerance

Complex ideas often require clear linguistic standards and a meticulous sentence structure. Vulgar varieties, lacking coherence to such standards, are unreliable for producing accurate expressions and transmitting precise thoughts. To equip a language with the necessary

IX. Diglossia & Digraphia

tools, linguists implement coding standards, which inevitably leads to a gap between colloquials and the new standardized form, or even the emergence of a new variety. Languages with minimal dialectal divergence may build a fully intelligible standardized model, maintaining monoglossia. However, when a multidialectal language with low mutual intelligibility, like Kurdish, creates a distinct H1 variety, the standardized form naturally differs from other dialects, leading to emerging diglossia. Indeed, no modern language has ever achieved perfect correspondence between vernaculars and a standardized form.

As the H1 variety is not natively spoken by any group, linguistic improvements such as changes in spelling, a reconceptualization of lexicon entries, and updates to grammatical rules are possible without disrupting colloquial norms. A degree of diglossia provides a lingua franca for interdialectal communication and reduces the need for bilingualism. When building new standards, if greater emphasis is placed on semantic details to achieve high precision, the standard model widens the lexical and grammatical gap between formal and vernacular varieties, resulting in lower comprehensibility and higher levels of diglossia. Conversely, if more importance is given to vernacular grammar and phonology, higher intelligibility between formal and vernacular varieties is preserved, yet the standards become less accurate. There are two poles: accuracy on one side and intelligibility on the other, where modern Kurdish must determine the balance, i.e., the scale level of diglossia. It is inevitable for a language with a large, dialectally diverse population, such as Kurdish and Arabic, to permit a wider gap between the standard and other varieties. For Kurdish to reach a state similar to Arabic and Chinese, it needs to tolerate an extended level of diglossia that includes a single classical Kurdish standard while preserving the spoken colloquial varieties.

The downside of diglossia is evident in the education system when young children struggle to adapt to the "school variety." For instance, a Sorani-speaking child may find learning in Sorani more efficient and beneficial in the early stages of education, while a Kurmanji-speaking child in Qamishli would find the codified Kurmanji better for acquiring knowledge. Thus, for other regions of Kurdish speakers, both dialects may be difficult and less appropriate. Codifying every single variety would create ideal conditions for the curriculum system, however, would deepen social partitioning and aggravate mutual unintelligibility.

9.1.2.1 Pluricentricity and Polyglossia

Public dissemination in both formal Kurdish is generally accepted within regions where each dialect predominates. By aligning the formal standards, such as Latinizing the Sorani alphabet and minimally unifying grammar and lexicon, Kurdish could achieve the status of a single pluricentric language. *Pluricentricity* involves the adoption of one formal variety with different localized sets of standardization (Clyne, 1992). This term describes international variations similar to the distinctions between American and British English, Chinese in China and Taiwan, German in Switzerland, Luxembourg, and Germany, and French in France versus Quebec. (*) Pluricentricity can serve as a transitional period until conditions are favorable for complete linguistic unification.

To promote the development of pluricentricity, it is essential to encourage the deployment of both Kurmanji and Sorani across all regions irrespective of the dominant spoken dialect, reaching an acceptable level of fluency in both formal standards by all Kurdish speakers, tolerating the apparition of extended diglossia that may occur (Fishman, 1967). This polyglossia involves the coexistence of two formal varieties: the majority-spoken formal dialect (H1), the secondary formal dialect (H2), and the local vernacular (L). For example, in the region of Kirkuk, Sorani would serve as H1, Kurmanji as H2, and the local vernacular of Kirkuk as L. In contrast, in Duhok, Kurmanji would be H1, Sorani H2, and the local colloquial variety as L.

The distribution of polyglossic publications aims to enhance the understanding of other dialects, such as Kurmanji in Erbil and Sorani

---

* Barbara Schuppler, Martine Adda-Decker, Catia Cucchiarini, Rudolf Muhr. An introduction to pluricentric languages in speech science and technology. Speech Communication. Volume 156, Jan 2024, 103007. ISSN 0167-6393.
https://doi.org/10.1016/j.specom.2023.103007.
(https://www.sciencedirect.com/science/article/pii/S0167639323001413)

in Amed. This requires a comprehensive acquisition plan to aid the public in achieving the desired standard. Meanwhile, achieving a pluricentric status necessitates further corpus planning, involving major or minor adjustments to spelling and grammatical rules, in addition to a practicable status plan.

9.2 Orthography

As the isolated emergence and development of dialects often lead to distinct phonetic systems, the evolutionary process may result in the fragmentation of a language into smaller sub-languages, and consequently, the division of a nation into sub-nations. Orthography, as a writing system encompassing conventional across-dialectal rules, regulates the correspondence between phonemes and graphemes.

By preserving word spellings and maintaining phonological and lexical structures across language varieties, orthography plays a crucial role in sustaining the unity of vocabulary and language structure, and above all, retaining a higher level of mutual intelligibility. Moreover, it extends the lifespan of a language across generations and protects it, to a high degree, from decomposition and the emergence of sub-languages.

Jaine P. Stark, (2010, pp. 3-7) building on research by Williamson (1984) and Barnwell (1998), proposed that the development of an orthography should adhere to five principles: accuracy, acceptability, consistency, harmonization, and convenience. Jonathan Clarkson and Elena Iurkova further detailed these principles as follows:

- ✓ **Accuracy**: An orthography must adequately reflect the phonetic structures of the language.
- ✓ **Consistency**: An orthography should operate in a predictable manner such as transparent phoneme-grapheme representation and using regular morphological patterns

where changes in spelling follow predictable rules, based on changes in phonology.
- ✓ **Convenience**: Writers and publishers should be able to easily produce documents.
- ✓ **Harmonization**: Where established written codes in neighboring languages address similar linguistic phenomena, their methods of representation can be adopted.
- ✓ **Acceptability**: If the orthography is liked and used by the people, it is deemed acceptable. (*)

In addressing Kurdish dialectal variation, negotiating accuracy is conceivable, given that no single dialect is considered the generic standard. The current Kurdish orthographies for both Sorani and Kurmanji were designed with a high degree of accuracy; however, this precision has failed to maintain linguistic unity. Therefore, a preferable approach might be to consolidate different phonetic sources into one phonological structure, represented by a less accurate but unified system of orthography.

Orthographic Accuracy

Most Western linguists advocate for phonetic accuracy. The British philologist Henry Sweet (1845-1912) defined language as primarily a phonetic tool, emphasizing the significance of sounds. When a specific dialect is chosen as the standard, its oral characteristics are used as the basis for creating a phonemic formal variety, as exemplified by Italian:

> *"Language is the expression of ideas by means of speech-sounds combined into words. Words are combined into sentences, this combination answering to that of ideas into thoughts."*

Emphasizing phonetics, he added:

---

* Clarkson, Jonathan & Iukova, Elena. Important Factors in the Development of an Orthography Shin-Shorsu Rutul – a Case Study. SIL Forum for Language Fieldwork. December 2015 – 002, p 12

IX. Diglossia & Digraphia

"Phonetics is to the science of language generally what mathematics is to astronomy and the physical science. Without it, we can neither observe nor record the simplest phenomena of language" (Sweet, 1899)

Conversely, linguists in the 20th century, reflecting the noticeable increase in written communication, have shown a tendency to prioritize formal language forms over colloquial ones, with an emphasis on semantics and grammatical rules at the expense of phonetics. Ludwig Wittgenstein (1889-1951) introduced a new definition of language, de-emphasizing the role of sounds and focusing more on the meaning of words. Similarly, in this context, Professor Noam Chomsky (1965, p. 16) favors syntax over phonetics:

"The syntactic component of a grammar must specify, for each sentence, a deep structure that determines its semantic interpretation and a surface structure that determines its phonetic interpretation. The first of these is interpreted by the semantic component; the second, by the phonological component."

9.2.1 Digraphia

The use of more than one writing system for the same language is referred to as digraphia. A language may employ multiple orthographies for cultural, religious, or political reasons throughout its history. Many languages have been standardized in more than one orthographic system. Examples include Azeri, Uzbek, and Bosnian (which synchronously use Cyrillic and Latin scripts), and Turkish (which has used Arabic and Latin scripts diachronically). In such cases, each system often develops a distinct spelling and even syntactical system. When each orthographic system identified by a different name, may lead others to perceive them as distinct languages, misrepresenting identity by calling the same language different names to denote different languages, as seen with 'Urdu' and 'Hindi' (with Urdu using Arabic-Persian and Hindi Devanagari script), and Persian's names 'Dari' and 'Tajiki' (with the former using Arabic-Persian and the latter using Cyrillic script).

Therefore, unlike diglossia, digraphia perpetuates linguistic differences and, in the absence of a single formal variety, as with Kurdish, it increases dialectal isolation among speakers. This leads to the gradual divergence of sub-languages, driving dialects further apart. In the case of Kurdish, where digraphia is associated with diglossia and divided by international borders, it can easily indicate two different languages. Currently, Kurdish dialects use different writing systems contemporaneously and rely on different sources of loan words, such as Turkish in the north, Persian and Azeri in the east, and Arabic in the south.

9.2.2 Diorthographia

Unlike digraphia, which means the use of more than one script, *diorthographia* is associated with more than one orthography while written in the same script, where each orthographic system employs different formal forms of the language, such as different spellings of the same word. It is simply the coexistence of dual orthography within the same script. An example of a diorthographic language is English, where many words have different spellings in American and British forms.

A similar approach to modifying Kurdish is feasible by unifying the script while retaining the spelling variations. For instance, creating a Sorani dictionary in Latin or a Kurmanji dictionary in Arabic-Sorani while allowing locally preferred spellings. This method provides a flexible preliminary solution that does not require intensive large-scale efforts and encourages greater engagement with interdialectal spelling forms. For example, the word 'water' can be written as 'Av' (Kurmanji) and 'Aw' (Sorani) depending on the text dialect. A Kurmanji speaker would find 'Aw' easier to read than 'ناو' as it appears in the current Sorani script, additionally, will have the option to select either the corresponding form of their dialect, 'Av' or the equally right cognate 'Aw'.

IX. Diglossia & Digraphia

9.2.3 Defective Orthography

For centuries, Kurdish primarily existed as an oral language without an associated writing script. The orthographic systems currently in use were only developed in the early twentieth century when a decision was made to adopt Arabic and Latin-based alphabets. These systems, however, do not derive from Kurdish linguistic characteristics and fail to align perfectly with its phonological structure. Consequently, compromises were necessary to ensure that the spelling of words accurately reflected their sounds, with each grapheme precisely representing the corresponding phoneme. For instance, the Arabic short vowels marked by the diacritics (الضمة short U ' ُ ' /ʊ/ as in '*Should*', الكسرة short I ' ِ ' /ɪ/ as in '*Bit*', and الفتحة short A ' َ ' /ə/ as in '*Say*') were replaced by the letters و, ي, and ە respectively to emulate the traditional Western spelling method, aiming for high transparency.

This strict adherence to phonology has made Sorani spelling more accurate than Arabic in representing sounds. However, it has also limited the formal variety to a specific local dialect, confined to a small geographic area, rather than generalizing it to create a common nationwide cross-dialectal form. This geographic limitation has become more pronounced with the expansion of media and the increased engagement with different dialects.

On the other hand, *defective orthography*, where symbols (letters) are insufficient to represent all phonemes and allophones, although it creates an opaque language that is more challenging for young pupils, illiterates, and the uneducated to learn, broadens the linguistic landscape by incorporating a wider range of pronunciations into a single formal variety capable of accommodating diverse pronunciation forms. Transparency is more suitable for languages with low populations, limited dialectal diversity, and non-isolated communities. In contrast, Kurdish, with its larger population and greater dialectal diversity, benefits more from defective orthography, which simplifies pronunciation obstacles, allows graphemes to represent most allophones within a phoneme, preserving the visual representation of words in a generic cross-dialectal form, and contributes to language unity.

This principle is illustrated by the Arabic use of diacritics instead of short vowels. Using the letters و, ا, and ي (W, A, and Y), due to their capacity to represent a wider range of allophones is more beneficial for Sorani than the current system. For example, the Arabic word بيت (bait /beɪt/), Eng. house, omits the short vowel /e/, representing the diphthong /eɪ/ with the long vowel /j/, resulting in the spelling B, Y, and T. This approach maintains spelling unity across different dialectal pronunciations, such as Lebanese /beɪt/, Iraqi /bɪət/, and Egyptian /biːt/, without causing linguistic fragmentation. In contrast, Kurdish spelling systems cannot accommodate such diversity, as transparent orthography would require multiple spellings for different pronunciations, undermining lexical unity.

This evidence suggests that focusing on transparency—writing the exact sounds—suits individual dialects better than the language in its inter-dialectal form. Therefore, a widespread multi-dialectal language like Kurdish, which lacks an authoritative body to enforce a unified classical language, would benefit more from the Arabic (and Hebrew) model similar to Pahlavi writing, rather than the transparent Turkish model currently followed by both Sorani and Kurmanji.

9.2.4 Deep Orthography

Deep orthography (see Section 6.2) encourages readers to process printed words by referring to their morphology through the visual-orthographic structure at the expense of phonology. This approach allows certain graphemes to represent a wider range of allophones and even accommodate phonemes that vary across dialects. For instance, a single letter could simultaneously replace the sounds of 'V' and 'W' to facilitate unifying the spellings of the (Kurm./Sor.) words such as "Av/Aw" Eng. 'water', "Nav/Naw" Eng. 'name', and "Slav/Slaw" Eng. 'hello' – that is by using a unique grapheme to replace both 'V' and 'W'. This method would preserve lexical unity while allowing speakers to pronounce the words according to their preferred dialect. The ability of a single letter to represent multiple phonemes can serve as a unifying factor, bridging dialectal gaps.

In contrast to the shallow orthography currently used in Kurdish, languages such as English, French, unvocalized Arabic, and Chinese,

IX. Diglossia & Digraphia

among others, have deep, complex orthographies that are highly irregular, with sounds that cannot be predicted from the spelling. This deep orthography was also chosen by Eliezer Ben-Yehuda in the late nineteenth century for modern Hebrew, favoring it over a more transparent system.

9.2.5 Unified Dictionary

To achieve lexical unity, it is essential to establish a common reference for spelling in both the Arabic-Persian script, for the use of Sorani, and the Latin for the users of Kurmanji. The priority should not be to determine which system is more appropriate, but to unify the lexicon across both, and, if feasible, a script inspired by the historical Kurdish language, such as a modernized Pahlavi. This task involves creating a single Arabic-Persian script dictionary that etymologically combines and integrates both varieties into a unified lexicographic list, and similarly, producing a Latin dictionary that amalgamates the spellings of both formal varieties.

For instance, the word for "water" should appear as both "Aw" and "Av" as synonyms, in a single Latin dictionary, allowing them to be used interchangeably in texts, with no dialectal preference. At the same time, the words ئاڤ and ئاو listed together in an Arabic-Persian dictionary. Thus, a Kurmanji document may use either "Av" or "Aw," and a Sorani may use either ئاڤ or ئاو without distinction. These two resources should be regarded as the authoritative sources for formal communication.

Also, it would contradict unification efforts if certain lexemes were given priority over others within the related script. In other words, the Latin version should not give an advantage to the Kurmanji cognate *"Av"* (Eng. Water), *"Çima"* (Eng. Why), and *"Balafirgeh"* (Eng. Airport) at the expense of the Sorani *"Aw"*, *"Boçî"* and *"Frokexane"* Just because it already exists in the Latin form, nor similar preference to Sorani cognates in Arabic-Persian dictionary.

9.2.5.1 System Selection

After utilizing Arabic-Sorani to establish the spelling of Kurmanji cognates and Latin script for Sorani, the subsequent step involves selecting the most appropriate orthographic system.

Many scholars advocate for the Latin for several reasons:

1. Used by the majority of Kurdish speakers and is formally adopted in areas controlled by the Rojava authorities.

2. Prevalent in many of the world's major languages, facilitating the learning of Western languages that are rich in scientific and technological resources.

3. Adopted by languages of Indo-European origin, such as Germanic and Latin.

4. Available with marks and diacritics to suit Kurdish phonological characteristics.

5. Offers a variety of vowel letters and diphthongs.

6. Contains better resources as European scholars were the first to study Kurdish phonemes scientifically, inspiring Kurdish scholars, particularly in Armenia in 1928 and by Celadet Bedirxan a decade later.

7. The Arabic script has not thrived as a formal system despite being used for the first Kurdish newspaper "Kurdistan" (كردستان) in 1898.

8. Emancipates Kurdish from the Arabic influence imposed by religious and linguistic intersections.

However, proponents of the Arabic script argue for its use due to several factors:

1. As a liturgical script, it holds a revered status among Muslims, being the approved script for holy texts and religious rituals.

2. It is imposed by the central governments in Iran, Iraq, and Syria, where many Kurdish speakers reside.

3. The dominance of the Arabic script in the Middle East facilitates learning contiguous languages.

IX. Diglossia & Digraphia

4. The script is officially used in administrative communications between local Kurdish departments and central governments, especially within the region of Iraqi Kurdistan.

Regionally, using a writing system similar to that of the country facilitates language acquisition, which is vital for tourism and administrative communication. Thus, speakers might prefer one script over another for subjective reasons (such as fluency) or objective (such as business requirements and the administrative system of their country).

Coining a unified dictionary requires a harmony of *practical* and *theoretical* lexicographers. While theoretical lexicographers provide the semantic and orthographic presentation of words and suggest exemplary sentences for newly crafted syntagms, practical lexicographers create a standard form of lexemes, compiled in lemma order and including dialectal inflection diversity. These cooperative efforts of both practical and theoretical lexicographers, determine the selection of loanword replacements, the elimination of rare synonyms, and the coining of new terms.

9.2.5.2 Variation of Cognates

Notwithstanding a large proportion of cross-dialectal cognates share the same sound, such as 'Ba' 'با' Eng. 'Wind' and 'Kur' '' Eng. 'Son', the dual formality produces other proportions that differ at various levels:

1. Vowel bias: Two cognates stem from the same morphemes but a vowel may slightly sound different, like:
    - Kurm. 'Asûman' /aːsʊman/, Sor. 'ناسمان' /aːsman/, Eng. 'Sky'.
    - Kurm. 'Jîyan' /ˈʒɪjaːn/, Sor. 'ژیان' /ʒjaːn/, Eng. 'Life'.
    - Kurm. 'Xwîn' /ˈxwɪjːn/, Sor. 'خوێن' /ˈxwen/, Eng. 'Blood'.

2. Consonant bias: Two cognates share the same morpheme but differ in consonant phoneme, Like:
    - Kurm. 'Stêrk' /stɪərək/, Sor. 'ئەستێرە' /əstɪərə/ Eng. 'Star.
    - Kurm. 'Girê' /gɪre/, Sor. 'گرد' /gɪrd/, Eng. 'Hill'.
    - Kurm. 'Nimêj' /nɪmɪəʒ/, Sor. 'نوێژ' /nɪwɪəʒ/.Eng. 'Prayer'.

3. **Consonant bias:** Two cognates derived from unalike morphemes, Like:
- Kurm. 'Pirsegirêk', Sor. 'کێشە' /kɪəʃə/ Eng. 'Problem'.
- Kurm. 'Lebê', Sor. 'بەڵام' /bəˈlɑːm/ Eng. 'But'.
- Kurm. 'Çem', Sor. 'ڕووبار' /rʊbɑr/ Eng. 'River'.

Selecting a minimal number of words from the given synonyms reduces redundancies, yet it involves lexicographers in intensive efforts in corpus linguistics. Additionally, prioritizing the selection criteria requires extensive discussion, where the decisions depend on potential debates among proponents of different dialects.

9.2.5.3 Scope of Dictionary

Selecting words for a unified dictionary depends on the scope of inclusion, which can be planned either to encompass all words from all dialects or to restrict based on certain criteria.

The scope plans could be:

1. **Inclusive:** This approach includes all synonyms, such as Kurmanji 'Sêv' and Sorani 'Sêw' Eng. 'apple', treating them as separate entries equally available for formal communication. The inclusive dictionary prioritizes pronunciation over spelling and may include all words from all varieties or restrict selection to those formally used in Kurmanji and Sorani.

2. **Restricted:** This approach selects a single entry from synonymous words sharing the same root morpheme, such as choosing either 'Sêv' or 'Sêw', disregarding the other. Selection criteria might include ease of pronunciation, comprehensibility, origin, age, or other preferences.

3. **Practical:** This approach is restricted but allows for multiple entries of synonyms based on criteria such as widespread usage or other significant factors. Words with vowel bias can be approximated for a single entry while compromising on those with consonant variations. However, synonyms of different morphemes may be included as different entries.

IX. Diglossia & Digraphia

9.3 Phonology

Humans can produce an estimated 800 phonemes. However, languages vary in the number of available ones, and different language varieties may possess more or fewer than others. Additionally, allophones change over time, leading to shifts in phonetic patterns primarily due to environmental factors, which result in the evolution of new accents. For instance, in a physically intensive lifestyle involving long-distance communication, the bilabial phoneme 'B' or the nasal 'M' might shift to 'OO' or 'V', to facilitate airflow by opening the mouth for better air passage. Repeated over time, this practice can create new phonetic patterns, causing the phonemes /b/ and /m/ to gradually shift to /u/ or /v/. Similarly, other phonemes may undergo changes, such as /z/ shifting to /ʒ/, and the final phoneme /d/ disappearing from some words.

Diachronic bias significantly influenced the evolution of Kurdish. For example, the Pah. 'Şeb' Eng. 'Night' evolved into Sor. 'Şew' and Kurm. 'Şev', and the Pah. 'Nîm' Eng. 'Half' transformed into Sor. 'Nîw' and Kurm. 'Nîv'. Integrating the diverse Kurdish varieties into one orthographic system involves merging multiple phonetic forms of a word to produce a single standard pronunciation. This can be approached in several ways:

1. **Inclusive Dictionary**: Index all words as multiple entries in a combined dictionary, where all spellings of 'Eye' ('Çav', 'Çaw', and 'Çem') are listed as formally correct with no preference.

2. **Single Key Selection**: Choose a single preferred spelling while excluding others. For instance, only allow 'Çaw' and consider 'Çav' and 'Çem' as colloquial. Persian addresses this by using the letter 'و', pronounced as 'V' in Iran and 'W' in Afghanistan (e.g., جوان 'Jawan' sounds 'Javan' in Iran and 'Jawan' in Afghanistan).

3. **Diacritic Marking**: Mark the disputed grapheme with a diacritic above or below the letter, such as tilde (õ), caron (ŏ), circumflex (ô), underdot (o̤), under-comma (o̦), or underbar (o̱). For example, using a tilde, the word can be formally accepted in the forms of 'Çaṽ', 'Çaw̃', and 'Çem̃'. This also helps distinguish homonyms, such as 'Çem̃' from Kurmanji 'Çem' (river).

4. **Auxiliary Modifier**: Selecting a modifier (for example 'Ĭ') to precede the target letter, so 'Eye', for instance, can be written as 'Çaĭv', 'Çaĭw', and 'Çeĭm', allowing the writer to choose the spelling based on their preferred dialect. An example is the Russian modifiers 'Ъ', 'Ь', and 'Ы', which alter the pronunciation of a preceding consonant or a following vowel.

5. **New Letter**: Using a new letter to represent each of the sounds 'V', 'W', and 'M' in synonymous words. For example, coining a letter such as 'Λ' would allow the unifying 'Çav', 'Çaw', and 'Çam' in a single written form 'Çaл'. The unified form of a word not only accommodates dialectal pronunciations but assists speakers in anticipating the pronunciation form of the word in other dialects.

By adopting one of these strategies, Kurdish can achieve greater lexical unity and facilitate cross-dialectal written communication.

9.3.1 Grapheme-Phoneme Balance

To achieve maximum correspondence between phonemes and graphemes, both Sorani and Kurmanji dialects were synthesized into phonemic orthographies, ensuring that spelling aligns closely with pronunciation. This transparency is more suitable for homogenous languages with high inter-dialectal intelligibility, but not for languages with diverse variations. As Kurdish is rich in varieties and spoken over a vast region, it requires a certain degree of opacity rather than a strictly phonemic system. Transparent orthography, designed to reflect exact phonetics, tends to align with one particular variety, rather than serving as a universal standard. Conversely, opaque systems allow graphemes to cover a broader range of sounds,

IX. Diglossia & Digraphia

enabling alphabet characters to represent multiple shades of allophones or even different phonemes. This expansion allows the writing system to integrate dialectal diversity and approximate semantics in a comprehensive orthography.

A multi-dialect language with low inter-dialectal intelligibility, such as modern Arabic, benefits from defective orthography. The formal *Al-Fusṣha* is not tied to any specific spoken dialect but preserves a historic form, essentially making it dialect-free. This flexibility allows speakers to opt for the nearest suitable phoneme. For example, the Arabic word 'دور' /deör/ Eng. 'Turn', is written in modern classics as D, W, and R, ignoring the short vowel diacritics. This enables speakers from different regions to pronounce it differently—/dɔr/ in the Persian Gulj, /duːr/ in Egypt, and /daör/ in Lebanon—while maintaining a unified written form. The absence of equivalent letters for certain phonemes broadens the power of the existing vowels to encapsulate variant phonemes, thereby solidifying linguistic unity.

In contrast, Sorani orthography strictly follows vowel pronunciation, distinguishing 'O' 'ۆ' /ɔ/ from short 'U' 'و' /u/ and long 'U' 'وو' /uː/; the long 'A' 'ا' /aː/ from the short 'ە' /ə/, and the diphthong 'ێ' /ɪə/. It also differentiates consonants, such as 'L' 'ڵ' /ɫ/ and 'ل' /l/; and 'R' 'ڕ' /ɾ/ and 'ر' /r/. Based on the variety spoken in Sulaymaniyah, this orthographic system has left speakers of other dialects struggling with linguistic purism and discrimination.

The limitation of transparent orthography is its inability to accommodate phonetic changes over time, which is later widening the gap between phonemes and graphemes, thus the language eventually builds opacity. This natural modification is observed in some Western languages where spoken and written forms diverge over centuries. Consequently, Kurmanji and Sorani's writing systems may lose transparency in the foreseeable future, necessitating either spelling changes or increased opacity.

The strict structure of both Kurdish orthographies has contributed to linguistic division, prioritizing a local phonological status and alienating other dialects. This has prompted Gorani and southern dialects to develop their own writing systems.

By monitoring the worldwide successful linguistic projects, it is vital to exploit the modern Hebrew experience. Eliezer Ben-Yehuda, the father of modern Hebrew, recognized the limitations of extensive vowel use. He favored diacritics (Niqqud) for short vowels instead, similar to modern Arabic, where the word consists of a root and a morphemic pattern. Although Niqqud is largely neglected in modern writing, it is used in particular cases such as teaching the proper pronunciation, which is required in integrating immigrants, and in the early years of education. Thus, Hebrew maintains a dual-form orthographic system: one opaque for regular communication and one transparent for specific contexts.

9.4 Grammar

A lexical merger and the inclusion of equivalent synonyms do not imply that the language is fully unified or that the standard is intelligible for all speakers. Lexical similarity is one fundamental factor in mutual intelligibility between two varieties, thus, the unification of Kurdish cannot be achieved solely through a unified dictionary. Phonetic, morphological, and syntactical similarities are also essential for considering two varieties as mutually intelligible. For instance, the Ethnologue database indicates that Spanish has a lexical similarity of 82% with Italian, 85% with Catalan, and 89% with Portuguese. Despite the high rate of lexical similarity, mutual intelligibility with Portuguese is only estimated between 50% to 60%. (*) This demonstrates that high lexical similarity alone cannot create linguistic unity. To achieve comprehensibility, other factors such as grammatical, cultural, and sociolinguistic elements predominate. (†)

---

* Jensen, John B. "On the Mutual Intelligibility of Spanish and Portuguese." Hispania 72, no. 4 (Dec. 1989): 848–52. <https://doi.org/10.2307/343562>

† Jung, M-Y. "The Intelligibility and Comprehensibility of World Englishes to Non-Native Speakers", Journal of Pan-Pacific Association of Applied Linguistics, 2010, 14(2), 141-163.

IX. Diglossia & Digraphia

A meaningful sentence is more than just a sequence of words; it requires grammatical rules such as syntax and conjugation to convey meaning. For example, the word "car" by itself does not specify a particular car (as a physical entity) and does not answer questions like "which," "when," "where," "what size," or "what color." It does not provide any context or describe an event. Meaning is derived from grammatical rules that clarify sentence ambiguity. Grammar is a language-specific guideline for using syntax, punctuation, tenses, determiners, and connectors (De Saussure, 1959, p. 118). Since these rules are conventional, and not formulated by any law, there is always an opportunity for linguists to participate in adjusting and regulating them to synthesize and promote a single set of rules. The unified Kurdish grammar may also allow the readjusting of local grammar patterns and derive more advanced regulation.

9.4.1 Syntax

The syntax is a language-specific pattern that determines the order of words in sentence structure – that is, the position of the three main constituents: Subject (S), Verb (V), and Object (O), in addition to the adverbs and adjectives. For example, different languages follow distinct syntactic orders:

- English (SVO): As in "He calls you," where the subject 'He' precedes the verb 'calls,' which in turn precedes the object 'you.'

- Spanish (SOV): In "El te llama," the subject 'El' (he) comes first, followed by the object 'te' (you), and the verb 'llama' comes last. This order is also observed in Japanese and Persian.

- Arabic (VSO) and (SVO): Both syntactic orders are permissible, as seen in "هو يناديك" (He calls you) and "ينادي هو عليك" (Calls he you)

In addition, some languages follow different orders such as VOS, OVS, and OSV.

Kurdish syntax differs in Sorani and Kurmanji. The sentence in this example is written as:

Kurm.**SVO**   *"Ew gazî te dike".*   he -> call -> you

Sor. **VOS** *"پەیوەندیت بێوە دەکات"*.   call -> you -> he

Zaza **SOV** *"O to rê beno"*.   he -> you -> call

In vernacular varieties, syntactic structure is not as rigid as in the standard form. The meaning of a sentence may also rely on intonation, gestures, and local conventional order, which may differ from the standardized syntax. However, since variation in word order within Kurdish reflects its vernacular diversity, a unified syntax may need to adhere to a single order, as the position of a word determines its association with the subject or the object.

9.4.2 Tenses

Grammatical tenses categorize the time of an event as past, present, or future, usually relative to the moment of speaking. Verbs indicate a specific tense often through conjugation patterns that express the event's timing. For example, in most English verbs, adding 'ed' signifies the past tense. Yet, complexity arises when sentences reference different points on the timeline, distinct from the moment of speaking. This involves using relative moments in the past or future and expanding tenses to provide more details that occur before or after. For instance, languages can distinguish between a past time relative to another past moment (past perfect), a future time relative to a past moment (future in the past), and similarly, the past of a future and the future of a future. Furthermore, some languages consider verb aspects (perfective and imperfective) and verb moods, indicating the likelihood of an event in conditional sentences.

Given that time is a universal concept independent of language, one might expect a uniform number of tenses or a common pattern across all languages. However, languages vary significantly in how they reference time, the number of tenses, and conjugation patterns. Some, like Chinese varieties, Malay, and Burmese, are considered tenseless, meaning they do not refer to time through tenses. Others, like Arabic, use two forms to distinguish between past and nonpast (present and future) despite recognizing three temporal categories (past, present, and future).

IX. Diglossia & Digraphia

These grammatical approaches lead to different numbers of tenses. For example, Kurdish (Sorani) uses five tenses, German six, French eight, Persian nine, English twelve, and Spanish sixteen. Tenses are not standardized based on scientific principles but are constructed to balance phonological habits and eloquence while minimizing the learner's effort.

Since grammar comprises conventional rules, including those for tenses, linguists can refine these rules by adopting more suitable solutions, such as the unification of rules, to enhance clarity and coherence across dialects and languages.

9.5 Semantics

When we hear the word 'Dar' دار Eng. 'tree', the most prevalent sense is typically the one associated with trees commonly seen in parks and gardens. However, the term can also carry multiple additional meanings. The direct, *conceptual meaning*, encompasses the basic, essential components conveyed by the literal use of a word (Yule, G., 1985, p. 120). In contrast, human imagination often derives *associative meanings*. For instance, the rigidity of a tree inspired the Spanish poet Alejandro Casona to symbolize human tenacity in his 1949 play "*Los árboles mueren de pie*" [The Trees Die Standing]. The branching pattern of a tree resembles the expansion of families, leading to phrases like 'dara malbatê' (Sor. 'داری بنەماڵە' , Eng. 'family tree'), and its fruitfulness is associated with the wishes of Christmas.

<u>Conceptual meaning</u> denotes a tree as a physical entity, while <u>associative meanings</u> connote ideas such as sustainability, fruitfulness, and the green color.

These two types of meanings, conceptual and associative, require different approaches in the process of unification. The former requires a clear, unified standard definition in an approved dictionary. The latter, however, can vary depending on factors such as region, mood, and intention. Overlapping associative meanings can bias the concept in the absence of a stipulated definition. For example, the word 'Neck' connotates 'Responsibility' in Kurdish culture, similar to 'Shoulder.' Without a unified conceptual definition, the Kurmanji word 'Mil' obtained the meaning of 'shoulder', while its homophone 'مل' /'mɪl/ in Sorani and Pahlawani means 'Neck'. This semantic divergence suggests the influence of associative meanings on the conceptual framework.

Over time, shifts in meaning can alter word definitions. For instance, the Pahlavi term 'Kishwar' Eng. "region, clime, and continent" (MacKenzie, 1971) was inherited by Kurdish and Persian. While it retained its meaning as 'Continent' in Kurdish, it shifted to mean 'Country' in Persian. This shift might be attributed to the authoritative discourse of the Persian Empire, which aimed to connotate the empire's vastness, merging conceptual differences in the same inherited word.

Unifying the conceptual meanings and listing the associative can preserve lexicon stability, increase intelligibility, and enhance precision in cross-dialect communication.

X. Unification

> *"No two languages are ever sufficiently similar to be considered as representing the same social reality. The worlds in which different societies live are distant worlds, not merely the same world with different labels attached."*
>
> Edward Sapir (1929)

Language is more than a simple medium for conveying thoughts in bilateral conversations. Maintaining a high degree of cross-dialectal intelligibility plays a vital role in preserving national coherence, integrating regional diversity, and culturally aligning social traits. Conversely, a language lacking a unique standardized variety—where dialects are separately standardized—weakens the vast regional bonds, creates sub-languages, and fosters the pride of sub-ethnicity at the expense of national unity.

If Kurdish is not divided into semi-independent dialects, and all share a unified set of grammar and lexicon, it helps form a common national mindset. This unity can practically consolidate the basic structure of a nation (Alesina, Giuliano, Reich, 2018) across various domains such as politics, identity, beliefs, and even economic progress. As the Chinese linguist Yung You (2018, p. 3) stresses on the role of language in Nation-Building, Ideology, and Social Preferences:

> *"Language unification also unifies peoples' mindsets; speaking a common language nurtures their patriotism, strengthens national identity, and weakens local identity."*

A language shapes the contours of a nation and is the primary integrating feature among all others (race, religion, geography, territory, etc.). Thus, neglecting language unification allows sub-ethnic components to grow beyond controllable limits, resulting in further linguistic and consequently social partition. In other words, when a language is divided into multiple formal standards, sub-identities develop over time, making it challenging for forthcoming generations to maintain language integrity. This division imposes the burden of learning two sets of grammar and lexicon, effectively equating to learning two languages. Such dual linguistic forms can make national identity burdensome and frustrating for future generations.

For Kurdish intellectuals, language unification is ostensibly perceived as a purely cultural phenomenon and a mere linguistic obligation, often overlooking its social, economic, and political impacts. This perspective explains why politicians have not taken significant steps in this direction and why intellectuals have not actively raised public awareness regarding its importance. The efforts of KRG and the Autonomous Administration of North and East Syria are primarily focused on political disputes with central governments, often having other issues sidelined, thereby neglecting sociocultural development and its implications.

As the Kurdish language has not received adequate attention for decades, a large-scale project of major modification requires an advanced and supported linguistic body, with intensive efforts from a team of specialists covering various aspects of linguistics-related sciences.

In conclusion, language unification represents a highly valued strategic initiative, essential for maintaining national unity and warranting greater attention.

10.1 Scope of Unification

When cross-dialectal communication requires clarity, such as in official correspondence and nationwide announcements, a set of agreed-upon rules is essential to ensure precision. Thus, unification does not entail compelling Kurdish speakers to abandon their dialects in everyday conversations, nor does it involve convincing them to

X. Unification

modify their grammatical habits. The process is solely aimed at adopting a standardized set of grammar and lexicon within a specific type of language usage (registers).

10.1.1 Language Registers

In linguistic terms, a "register" refers to a variation of language used for a specific purpose or in a particular social setting (Halliday, 1978). Registers are influenced by factors such as the topic of conversation, the relationship between the speakers, and the context in which communication occurs. This concept acknowledges that language use can vary significantly depending on these factors, and different registers are suitable for different situations. The most common types of linguistic registers include:

- **Formal:** Used in professional, academic, or official settings. It involves standard grammar and vocabulary. For example, legal documents or academic papers.

- **Informal**: Used in casual or familiar settings. It may include colloquial language, slang, and contractions. For example, text messages or conversations with friends.

- **Technical**: Specific to particular fields or professions, using jargon and specialized terms. For example, medical reports or engineering manuals.

- **Consultative**: Used in semi-formal situations where interaction requires clarity but is not overly formal. For example, teacher-student interactions or business meetings.

- **Frozen**: Language that is fixed and ritualistic. Often found in religious texts, legal oaths, and national anthems.

- **Intimate**: Used in private communication between close individuals, often involving personal language and expressions. For example, conversations between spouses or close family members.

It is imperative to inform the public, particularly proponents of linguistic purity, that the process of language unification does not encompass informal, consultative, and intimate registers or colloquial varieties. This initiative does not seek to promote the use of one dialect over another in everyday interactions. The unification of the language is solely aimed at standardizing formal which may be extended to technical and frozen registers in a later course of time but does not impinge upon the freedom to use existing dialects in any way.

10.2 Why Unification

Facilitating internal communication can significantly boost the economy by increasing investment opportunities and fostering a more cohesive regional culture. A unified media language can elevate local issues to the national level, garnering broader advocacy and support. In essence, language unification promotes not only national unity but also patriotic orientation. In the long term, it is a crucial step toward the rebirth of Kurdish identity as a nation. It underscores the necessity of prioritizing national unity above regional interests, as it empowers the media to mobilize political forces and mitigate the dispersion of loyalties.

10.2.1 Role of Media

The influence of media on contemporary society has surpassed its traditional role of providing information, evolving into a powerful force that shapes lifestyles, especially in key areas such as the economy and politics. Media now possesses the ability to dictate consumer choices, from hair dye to shoe color, and to influence social norms and election trends.

Since the establishment of the first weekly newspaper, The Boston Evening Post, in 1770, and the subsequent expansion of print media

X. Unification

in America during the 1830s, media has become *"an actual or potential adversary of established power, especially in its own self-perception"*. (McQuail, par 2.2)

In recent days, with the advancement of modern technology over the past few decades, media has played a decisive role during critical historical events, such as the collapse of the Eastern Bloc in 1991 and the Arab Spring in 2011. Today, it can target individuals at work, on public transport, and in their bedrooms via smartphones, contributing to the formation of a unified collective consciousness. It connects and integrates a diversity of regional and varied human resources, and it is the most influential factor in the dissemination of modern cultural norms, political advocacy, and religious doctrines.

Beyond raising awareness about social issues and driving societal changes, the media industry generates substantial market profits. For instance, the global television market revenue in 2022 alone amounted to approximately 94 billion U.S. dollars. (*)

However, media can also be manipulated to steer society toward conflict or non-democratic rule, as highlighted in a special report by the United States Institute of Peace:

"In contrast to active use of media outlets to promote conflict, media can also contribute to conflict involuntarily. Such passive incitement to violence most frequently occurs when journalists have poor professional skills, when media culture is underdeveloped, or when there is little or no history of independent media. Under such circumstances, journalists can inflame grievances and promote stereotypes by virtue of the manner in which they report, even though their intentions are not necessarily malicious and they are not being manipulated by an outside entity. Such a scenario is less common than that in which media are actively manipulated, but it is no less dangerous." (Frohardt & Temin, 2003, p. 2)

The main tool exploited by media is language. Thus, advanced linguistics significantly influences in various ways, enhancing

---

[*] statista.com/topics/4999/television-industry-worldwide/#topicOverview

communication, improving accessibility, and shaping content to better engage audiences.

10.2.1.1 Unified Kurdish In Mass Media

The size of the audience in modern visual media directly correlates with various factors: the broader the audience, the more advantageous and influential the media becomes. The number of fluent language speakers who can readily understand the delivered content boosts outcomes in terms of economic impact, social engagement, and political mobilization. However, a language fraught with inconsistencies would fall short of meeting the requirements for successful dissemination.

Mass media operates far more effectively with rich, powerful, and widely spoken languages.

The unification of a standardized Kurdish would provide the necessary means to potentially double the audience. Beyond economic feasibility, this unification would enable the media to address the entire nation, ultimately contributing to the blurring of socio-cultural boundaries (Kustiawan, Erwan Efendi, Arfah, Zul Akbar Shah, 2022) and creating a unified stance on critical national issues.

In May 1995, the era of Kurdish-speaking satellite television was inaugurated by Med TV. Viewers from all Kurdish-speaking regions began, for the first time, to follow multi-dialectal programs, collectively experiencing influential discourse from a single political entity. The policy of assimilating dialects succeeded in attracting and influencing audiences from various dialectal backgrounds, thereby transferring political sympathy from local issues to those of a general national nature.

The role of language in supporting media, in general, is exemplified by the success of the Qatari Al Jazeera Television Network. Shortly after its launch in 1996, despite Qatar's population being barely over half a million, it managed to expand its everyday viewership to 35 million by the year 2000, Without utilizing widespread formal Arabic, the broadcast would have been confined to the local Persian Gulf vernacular, limiting the audience to thousands.

X. Unification

A widely spoken formal language does not only benefit the promotion of political stances. An eloquent language also broadens and enhances the role of media in daily life. For example, English-language mass media, including online websites, has significantly advanced its influence on social life due to the language's simplicity and ease of comprehension. This has allowed for an expanded field in politics and the entertainment market, education, and e-government.

10.2.1.2 Challenges of Kurdish Media

Highlighting the positive aspects does not imply that the role of media is devoid of negative influences on social norms and beliefs. It can manipulate, influence, and pressurize society in both positive and negative ways.

Kurdish, lacking the standard capabilities to compete with other major languages in the Middle East, leaves social norms vulnerable to counter-media and intrusive attempts to engineer the social mindset. Turkish channels, for instance, have adopted an indoctrinating policy that manipulates terminology concerning Kurdish peculiarities. Examples include name replacements, such as avoiding the use of "Kurdistan" and substituting it with designations like "southeastern Turkey," "northern Iraq," and "northern Syria." Additionally, political forces advocating for cultural rights are labeled as "terrorists".

Kurdish media has also not reached the level of competition necessary to rival its Arabic counterparts. In 2015, while there were only a few dozen Kurdish satellite channels, there were 1,230 Arabic, excluding foreign-based broadcasts. (*)

The third major competitor in attracting Kurdish viewers is the state-supported Persian media. This multitude of diverse outlets, produced by advanced facilities and supported by extensive

---

* [1230 Arabic stellite channels قناة مجموع القنوات الفضائية العربية لعام 20151230] in 2015]. Al Eqtisadiah (9 Jul 2016). (Dialy newspaper). 8307, Riyadh <web.archive.org/web/20160813035217/http://www.aleqt.com/2016/07/09/article_1068919.html>

experience in drama production, has proven influential in directing public opinions.

Despite these challenges, Kurdish media holds vast opportunities in both public and private sectors for stimulating the economy, raising public awareness, and regulating social norms. Achieving this potential requires advanced professionalism in production and the use of comprehensive and well-perceived language for public interaction.

10.2.1.3 Political Advance

Traditionally, one of the initial steps taken by a military coup is to control the media. Following the seizure of the presidential palace and the defense ministry, the coup plotters often target the Radio and Television complex. This strategy predated the advent of social media, where platforms like Twitter and Facebook have played pivotal roles in major political events over the last decade. This underscores the significant utilization of media for political purposes.

Given the previously discussed enhancement of the media's influential role through language unification, it is evident that political entities can derive substantial benefits from language standardization. For instance, despite its small size and population of Qatar, it has attained a significant position in Middle Eastern and Arab political affairs largely through the effective use of media in standard Arabic. This strategy has enabled the country to reach a broad audience across the Arab world, fostering a unified stance on major political issues. In contrast, a provincial television station like "Gali Kurdistan" in Sulaymaniyah, which fails to incorporate multi-dialectal outlets, is limited to promoting a regional political perspective. This limitation inaugurates local political and cultural sectarian isolationism, as the station can only target an audience that speaks a specific dialect in a certain region.

An advanced media apparatus can promote social cohesion, whereas inadequate performance can exacerbate divisions and entrench sectarian cultures. Despite access to modern technology in Kurdish regions, challenges remain in effectively disseminating crucial information. For instance, many Kurds in "North Kurdistan" are unaware that millions of "Faili" Kurds were expelled from

X. Unification

southern Iraq to Iran during the 1970s and 1980s. This lack of awareness persists despite dedicated activities, seminars, and the Iraqi Parliament's recognition of the Faili Kurds' deportation as an act of genocide. This gap in knowledge is not due to indifference or insufficient solidarity but rather a lack of a common communication medium, an intelligible variety that actually functions in both regions, highlighting the need for a unified standard Kurdish language.

The poor linguistic status also affects other Kurdish populations under Iraqi authority, such as those in Kirkuk, Khanaqin, and Shingal, who struggle to connect effectively with Kurds in eastern regions. For example, in January 2014, during the ISIS invasion of Kobani, global media attention and solidarity efforts pressured the USA and the West to compel Turkey to allow aid, resulting in a historic victory. In contrast, during the Turkish invasion of Afrin in 2019, public solidarity was markedly weaker despite similar circumstances. This disparity in reaction was due to the poor performance of Kurdish media. While Kobani benefited from global media support, Afrin's plight was largely confined to narrow discourse, hindered by the lack of a unified standard language. Consequently, Kurdish viewers often resort to Turkish, Persian, or Arabic media, which are not impartial and tend to reflect their respective national agendas.

The impact of Arabic media is particularly evident in southern Kurdish regions, where it has successfully framed Kurdish rights as excessive demands. This influence has extended to prominent Kurdish politicians, such as parliamentarian Mrs. Ala Talabani, who in a 2016 interview with Al-Iraqia television, called for the Iraqi army to recapture Kirkuk from Kurdish forces, accusing the Kurdistan ruling party of illegally exploiting oil resources. Her remarks aligned with Baghdad's efforts to mobilize support for the subsequent military campaign in October, which aimed to reassert control over the province and initiate a new phase of Arabization.

10.2.2 Culture

Language is often regarded as the identity of a nation, while culture is considered its character. It establishes unique qualities based on the reservoir of language, encompassing folk tales, mythologies, and an extensive list of historical scripted events. Language serves as a tool for culture to reproduce itself and transmit traditions across generations; consequently, a well-maintained language enriches the socio-cultural experience. In contrast, neglecting language maintenance can disrupt the genuine cultural diachronic flow, isolating newer generations from their intellectual legacy.

The loss of mythology, for instance, results from not preserving a robust orthography capable of transmitting words across generations. The costly consequence is not merely the abandonment of valuable roots but also the risk of appearing as a nation without history. Furthermore, neglecting the necessity of dialectal intelligibility creates internal cultural barriers, which is a primary cause of national fragmentation. Over time, various unconnected forms of culture and lifestyle weaken the spirit of a common national identity.

The unification of formal linguistic standards bridges the gap, converging disparate sub-cultures into a cohesive mainstream. The subsequent cultural unity not only enhances internal communication among the nation's segments but also positively influences all social aspects. It reinforces strong interrelationships, harmonizes concepts, and solidifies the essence of common thoughts.

10.2.3 Economy

Fluent communication, facilitated by linguistic cohesion profoundly solidates social structure, lays the foundation for a vibrant economic environment, and significantly boosts the national economy. It enhances the growth of internal investment, trade, and marketing (Mkwinda-Nyasulu, 2013).

For instance, proficiency in Kurdish is crucial for an investor from Duhok to establish a firm or engage in the marketing industry in Sulaymaniyah, and vice versa. Conversely, the lack of a common, coherent linguistic framework can result in disjointed economic sectors. The relationship between language and the economy is directly proportional; as language proficiency boosts economic growth, economic development, in turn, augments the use of the language. From the perspective of national identity, the vitality of a

X. Unification

language is intimately connected to its engagement in economic processes. A competent language gains higher economic value, while a less capable one may decline, potentially disappearing from the map of effective languages. For example, the global demand for Mandarin has surged due to China's flourishing economy. In 2021, over 70 countries incorporated the language into their national education curricula, with over 4,000 universities offering optional courses. According to Tian Xuejun, China's vice minister of education, an estimated 25 million students worldwide were learning Chinese as a second language. (*)

Typically, a fragmented language faces significant obstacles in expanding its reach and potential. Without a common formal dialect, this division hampers the development of a high-economic-value language. In South Kurdistan, particularly in Arbil and Sulaymaniyah, the Kurdish language has garnered attention since the early twenty-first century due to noticeable economic development and the influx of investors, manpower, and marketers from Iraq, regional countries, and even overseas. Consequently, there has been an increased interest in learning Kurdish, prompting universities worldwide to consider offering courses and notable institutions such as the University of Tokyo (Japan), SOAS University (England), and Bremen University (Germany) have started to provide. However, these institutions often face confusion due to linguistic fragmentation, forced to select a specific dialect, such as SOAS University, which offers lessons in the Kurmanji dialect, while Harvard University selected Sorani.

10.3 Examples of Unification

Most languages typically evolve from spoken vernaculars, gradually developing unique linguistic features. Over time, these

---

* Confucius Institute, Qufu City, 16 Dec 2020.
<http://www.kongziyjy.org/plus/view.php?aid=3356>

languages often undergo a process of unification, where a single standard variety is adopted for formal usage and refined to facilitate clearer communication. Prominent examples include French, Italian, and Spanish. For a non-standardized language like Kurdish, implementing a modernization project, and utilizing the latest advances in linguistics and related fields, is crucial. Fortunately, there is a wealth of expertise and proven methodologies available to guide the modification of Kurdish. Establishing an official body of specialists to analyze successful language standardization efforts from history could inform the creation of an effective strategy.

Among the various examples of language unification, the enhanced orthographic model of German, the logographic solution in Chinese, the coexistence of dual formality in Norwegian, and the promotion of a single dialect in Italian offer valuable insights. However, the extraordinary revival of Hebrew in the late 18th century, transforming it from a dead into an official language within a few decades, stands out as particularly noteworthy. This example underscores the potential for successful Kurdish unification and modernization when guided by well-planned and executed strategies.

10.3.1 The Chinese Solution

The status of the Chinese language is subject to controversy, as there is no unanimous linguistic consensus affirming its existence as a single language. According to Western linguistic standards, the various Chinese dialects are considered separate languages due to their lack of mutual intelligibility, suggesting that there is no single language known as "Chinese." However, from the perspective of the Chinese government, efforts to create a unified language form have been addressed through the adoption of a logographic writing system. This system enables mutual understanding across different dialects. The status was achieved by using symbols that convey meaning regardless of phonetic representation.

Unlike alphabetic orthography, the logographic system is not based on phonemes but on symbols that represent concepts or objects. Similar to cuneiform and hieroglyphics, a symbol like that for a house can be read in any language using different sounds while retaining

X. Unification

the same meaning. This method effectively bridges linguistic barriers, allowing people across China to communicate in writing even if they cannot understand each other's spoken conversation. By designating these varieties as dialects rather than separate languages, China has maintained national unity and cohesion under the umbrella of a distinct Chinese variety.

This approach to language unification has facilitated the integration of over a billion speakers of different dialects, contributing to national integrity. Consequently, China views multidialectal education as a threat to this unity.

The researcher Yang You (2018) explains:

"Nation-building over a multi-lingual and multi-cultural area is exceptionally challenging, and a potential collapse of the country is a persistent threat."

The Chinese success in merging several 'languages' into a single form inspires the Kurdish unification to contain its few dialects. However, despite its resounding achievement, the unification of the Chinese may not seem a feasible solution for Kurdish varieties for these reasons: With thousands of characters, the logography is far more complex than the alphabetic system used by Kurdish speakers, and ignoring the phonemes further deteriorates the level of intelligibility among Kurdish dialects, as well as making it hard to lay out an acquisition plan.

10.3.2 The Norwegian Solution

In Norway, the formal language encompasses two mutually intelligible written standards: Bokmål and Nynorsk. The origin of this duality dates back to the 18th century when the country was under the occupation of Denmark. During this period, Danish was the language of the urban educated class, while various Norwegian dialects were spoken in rural areas. Following Norway's independence in 1814, efforts were made to nationalize the language, leading to the development of *Bokmål* through gradual linguistic reforms influenced by Danish.

Subsequently, with the rise of nationalistic sentiments, Ivar Aasen, a philologist and lexicographer, created *Nynorsk* (New Norwegian) in the mid-19th century. Aasen's work was based on several rural dialects, aiming to establish a form that was as purely Norwegian as possible. His efforts culminated in the production of Nynorsk in 1836, following extensive linguistic research across Norway.

In addition to these official standards, two unofficial written forms emerged: *Riksmål*, a more conservative variant of Bokmål, and *Høgnorsk*, associated with Nynorsk. Although these dialects are mutually intelligible, their establishments are politically motivated rather than rooted in spoken variations.

In an attempt to unify these standards, a parliamentary debate was initiated in 1929 to merge both into a single standard called *Samnorsk*. However, this proposal failed to gain majority support, resulting in the continued coexistence of both standards. Currently, Bokmål is used by approximately 95% of Norwegian speakers. Both Bokmål and Nynorsk are employed in writing and formal communication, but neither is spoken in everyday conversation.

The key distinction between the use of dual standards in Norwegian and Kurdish lies in their geographical and ethnic contexts. While Norwegian speakers have the option to choose between Bokmål and Nynorsk within the same population, Kurdish speakers are geographically divided, with each dialect associated with distinct sub-ethnic groups. The concurrent use of Norwegian standards might be suitable for official use within the Kurdistan Regional Government (KRG) and self-ruled Northern Syria, i.e. the parallel use of both formal dialects in the same region for official and educational mainstream. However, the absence of a single Kurdish dialect may entrench the perception of the Kurds as a divided nation.

10.3.3 Unification of Italian

Modern Italian did not evolve until the country's unification in 1861. Before that, various regional dialects competed for dominance. The need for a unified language standard for administration and formal communication became apparent, especially fueled by the

X. Unification

post-war rise in patriotic sentiment. Tuscan, which was not only closest to vulgar Latin but also the primary dialect for literature since the 14th century, was selected as the formal Italian. This dialect had been used by eminent poets such as Dante Alighieri (1265-1321), Francesco Petrarca (1304-1374), and Giovanni Boccaccio (1313-1375).

The selection of Tuscan as the standard was well-received by educated Italians, who adopted this unifying variety. As literacy rates increased, many speakers abandoned their native dialects in favor of the national language. This trend expanded significantly in the latter half of the 20th century with the advent of television, which promoted the linguistic symbol of the nation.

The Italian model is a quintessential example of how a literary and formal language standard can be established. This approach is often considered for Kurdish unification, exemplified by the early 20th-century selection of the Sulaymaniyah dialect, similar to Tuscan, as a base for Kurdish, due to its rich literary tradition and clear linguistic rules.

This method of selecting an existing dialect for formal use has precedents in other countries. In France, the Parisian dialect (known as the Francien) expanded to form modern French. In Spain, the Castilian dialect was chosen as the formal Spanish by a political agreement between Queen Isabella of Castile and King Ferdinand of Aragon in the 15th century. A comparable process occurred in early 20th-century Armenia, where the eastern dialect was selected for a unified Armenian following the Ottoman genocide and the decline of the Western Armenian speakers.

These examples underscore the importance and success of selecting a prestigious and literarily rich dialect to serve as the foundation for a unified national language.

10.3.4 German Orthographic Unification

German, like Kurdish, is considered a pluricentric language due to the existence of different standardized variants in Germany, Austria, and Switzerland. In an effort to simplify and modernize the language, representatives from Germany, Austria, and Liechtenstein met in Vienna in July 1996 to agree on a new orthographic reform, which was later also adopted by Switzerland and Luxembourg. This reform aimed primarily at systematizing the correspondence between phonemes (sounds) and graphemes (letters), resulting in changes to spellings, adjustments to noun capitalization rules, and the separation of compound nouns.

In response to debates and protests, the Council for German Orthography (*Rat für deutsche Rechtschreibung*, RdR) was established in 2004 as a recognized authority for regulating standard orthographic structure. The council comprises 41 members representing the seven regions where German is spoken: Germany, Austria, Switzerland, Liechtenstein, Luxembourg, the South Tyrol province in Italy, and the German-speaking community in Belgium. The council approved the new spelling system on August 1, 2006, making it obligatory in all regions, officially adopted the capital ẞ (ẞ) letter in 2017, and issued the 25th version of the uniform German dictionary *Duden* in 2022.

Despite Kurdish also being a pluricentric, it has yet to receive an official unified dictionary. Following the German model, it is essential to establish an international body composed of members representing the four major Kurdish-speaking regions, as well as members from the Caucasus and North Khorasan province in Iran. The initial task would be to issue a unified language glossary using a preferred single writing system, thereby establishing a permanent linguistic body to harmonize dialects and unify and regulate standards.

10.3.5 The Rebirth of Hebrew

The successful process of reviving Hebrew from a dead liturgical to an everyday spoken, language among Israeli Jews is considered one of the most remarkable linguistic achievements in history. It began in earnest in the latter half of the nineteenth century, spearheaded by Eliezer Ben-Yehuda, originally Eliezer Yitzhak Perlman (1858–1922), a Russian linguist and lexicographer of the first modern Hebrew dictionary. It is widely believed that Ben-Yehuda initiated

X. Unification

the first modern Hebrew conversation with friends in Paris on October 13, 1881. By 1921, the language had gained recognition of official status in Palestine, and with the significant Jewish immigration to the region, it became the lingua franca for daily communication within the Jewish community. This revival transformed Hebrew from a solely liturgical into a spoken and literary language (Parfitt, 1983). During the British Mandate in Palestine (1920–1948), Hebrew was recognized as a co-official language alongside English and Arabic. After the establishment of Israel in 1948, maintained its official status alongside Arabic until 2018, when it was designated as the sole official of the state.

One approach to modernizing Kurdish could involve drawing inspiration from the revival of Hebrew and revisiting Pahlavi, the linguistic predecessor of Kurdish. Pahlavi's rich lexical reservoir preserves the roots of native morphemes and can help standardize the various cross-dialectal spellings and pronunciations. Just as Biblical and Mishnaic Hebrew contributed to the revival of modern Hebrew, with Ben-Yehuda expanding the lexicon from approximately 8,000 Biblical words to about 100,000, Pahlavi could similarly enrich modern Kurdish with native morphemes, original phonemes, affixes, and standardized word spellings, potentially providing an orthographic solution for a unified Kurdish writing system.

Hebrew and Pahlavi once coexisted as theological languages, with Hebrew eventually ceasing to be a living language and being preserved only for liturgical use in the holy books of Judaism. In contrast, Pahlavi became extinct after the Arab Muslim conquests and the decline of Zoroastrianism in the 7th century CE, though it remained in use for approximately two more centuries as a lingua franca in Persia and Mesopotamia. The distinction between Hebrew and Pahlavi underscores the crucial role of religion in safeguarding a language from extinction and fragmentation, as well as reviving it after it has become dead. This comparison highlights how religious continuity can serve as a powerful force in maintaining linguistic identity and facilitating language revival.

10.3.6 Evolution of Filipino

In an archipelagic nation like the Philippines, where over a hundred million native speakers communicate in 120-180 languages across more than seven thousand islands, establishing a single linguistic standard to unify the diverse populations was a challenging task that evolved gradually through extensive debate. The process of selecting a single dialect to be the only formal variety in the entire country took into consideration linguistic, social, and geopolitical factors, such as the prevalence of the classical language, its widespread use, and its association with modern urban lifestyles.

Ultimately, the standard language of the Philippines was chosen based on the Tagalog language, despite the Tagalog ethnic group not forming the majority of the population. At that time, the Visayan, which was the largest group, had not yet developed a unified formal dialect, mirroring the current situation of the Kurdish language. Their language was considered either a collection of low-intelligible dialects or several related languages. In contrast, Tagalog, representing the second largest group, was selected by the Philippines' national assembly to be the country's official; the key reason for this choice was the unity of its formal usage, which, after careful linguistic deliberation, was deemed essential to promoting a cohesive national language over the dispersed dialects of the majority group. The Philippine linguistic model highlights the importance of a unified formal dialect in the establishment of a national language, particularly in a linguistically diverse country. The major ethnic groups of the Philippines are illustrated in the following table. (*)

	Ethnicity	Population (in millions)
1	Visayan	31.1
2	Tagalos	22.5
3	Ilocano	8.1
4	Bicolano	6.2

* 2021 Philippines in Figures, Philippine Statistics Authority. pp. 23–24. ISSN 1655-2539

X. Unification

The highest population group *Visayan* is not considered an integrated ethnic group due to the linguistic variation which has undermined the ethnic unity. The language is divided into the following four main ethnolinguistics: (*)

	Group	Population (rounded to thousands)
1	Bisaya / Binisaya	15,523
2	Cebuano	8,684
3	Hiligayono / Ilongo	8,608
4	Waray	4,107

The historical development of Tagalog as the standard language can be traced back to its distinct geographical location. In the 17th century, the Spanish occupation chose Manila as their military center. The city's strategic position was crucial for defense against rivals such as the Dutch and the Portuguese.

Consequently, the language of Manila received significant attention and scholarly research, exemplified by the publication of the first Tagalog-Spanish dictionary, "*Vocabulario de la Lengua Tagala*" by Franciscan Pedro de San Buenaventura in 1613. The book with the subsequent contributions and edits over the centuries has further enriched the language.

This growing interest endowed Tagalog with the necessary semantic enhancement, the unity of standards, and practicality; ultimately making it a suitable choice for literary discourse and administrative communication.

Despite Spanish being the sole official language during the Spanish rule, the American occupation introduced English as a co-official. It was not until 1936 that the Institute of National Language was

---

* Ethnicity in the Philippines (2020 Census of Population and Housing) (7th Apr. 2023). Philippine Statistic Authority. Ref: 2023-77.
<psa.gov.ph/content/ethnicity-philippines-2020-census-population-and-housing>

established to select one of the native languages for official status. After a year-long survey, the Institute rejected the highest population and approved the second as the national language, citing five reasons for this decision, including the linguistic unity of Tagalog in contrast to the fragmented Visayan language(s).

The decision was implemented on July 4, 1946, coinciding with the Philippines' independence day.

Subsequent efforts to broaden the official language beyond Tagalog led to the inclusion of more vocabulary from other native languages and a name change to *Pilipino* in 1959, and later to *Filipino* in the constitutional amendment of 1973.

These efforts highlight the importance of a language as a symbol in fostering national identity and administrative efficiency.

"(2) The National Assembly shall take steps towards the development and formal adoption of a common national language to be known as Filipino." (*)

The promotion of Tagalog demonstrates the role of linguistic unity and its implication on the nation, it not only nominates the language for the status of official but maintains, along with the language, the ethnic identity. On the other hand, the historical neglect of the Visayan had led not only to the loss of the majority status but eventually to the segregation of their ethnicity.

The general census of 2020 displays how the unified Tagalog gained the majority by 26% above the divided Visayan groups despite that they collectively constitute a total of about 34% of the population.

The following table indicates the linguistic decline of the Vasaian in the light of ethnic division:

---

* Ethnicity in the Philippines (2020 Census of Population and Housing) (7th Apr. 2023). Philippine Statistic Authority. Ref: 2023-77.
<psa.gov.ph/content/ethnicity-philippines-2020-census-population-and-housing>

X. Unification

	Ethnicity	% of Population
1	Tagalog	26.0
2	Bisaya / Binisaya *	14.3
3	Ilcano	8.0
4	Cebuano *	8.0
5	Ilonggo *	7.9
6	Bikol / Bicol	6.5
7	Waray *	3.8
8	Kapampangan	3.0

(*) The groups of the Visayan.

Also, the Philippines' experience signifies the vital role of literature in language development, social stability, and ethnic integrity. The long neglect of Kurdish resembles the Visayan's decline in capability which has led to an ethnic rapture. On the other hand, the early lexical awareness and the efforts spent for Tagalog have not only maintained the linguistic capacity for a higher level of communication but remarkably promoted sociocultural models and factors. It has created a sense of integrated community.

Eventually, the unification of formal Kurdish could lift the language from the model of Visayan to the level of Tagalog.

Bibliography

Aflaq, Michel (1987). في سبيل البعث [*For the sake of Baath*]. Baghdad: Dar Al-Hurriah.

Akmeşe, Handan Nezir (2005), *The Birth of Modern Turkey: The Ottoman Military and the March to World War I*, London: IB Tauris.

Alesina, A., Giuliano P., Reich B. (2018). Nation-building and education. National Bureau of Economic Research Working Paper. No w18839

Anderson, Benedict R. O'G. (1991). *Imagined communities: reflections on the origin and spread of nationalism* (Revised and extended. ed.). London: Verso. ISBN 978-0-86091-546-1.

Asadi, Alireza (2012 [1392 AHSh]). فرهنگ تطبیقی گویش کردی ایلامی با زبان ایرانی میانه: پهلوی اشکانی، پهلوی ساسانی: به انضمام تاریخ و زبان استان ایلام قبل از اسلام [*Applied Dictionary of Ilami Kurdish Variety and Midde Iranic Language: Ashkanian Pahlavi and Sasanide Pahlavi Including Pre-Islam History and Language in Ilam Province*]. Ilam: Johar Hayat Publishing.

Azouri, Najib (1905). يقضة الأمة العربية [*The Awakening of the Arab Nation*]. Introduction by Qaddurah, Zahia. (

Barzun, Jacques, Salmon, John Hearsey McMillan, Weinstein, Donald, Treasure, Geoffrey Russell Richards, Stearns, Peter N., Mayne, Richard J., Sørensen, Marie-Louise Stig, Aubin, Hermann, Peters, Edward, Herlihy, David, Frassetto, Michael, Champion, Timothy C., Parker, N. Geoffrey and Herrin, Judith Eleanor. "History of Europe". Encyclopedia Britannica, 5 Mar. 2024.

<britannica.com/topic/history-of-Europe>

Bedirxan, Celadet (1994). Bingehen Gramera Kurdmancî [*Basic Kurdish Grammar*]. Weşanen Nûdem, ed. 1.

Bedirxan, Celadet. (1934); حول المسألة الكردية، قانون إبعاد وتشتيت الأكراد [*On the Kurdish issue, Law of deportation and dispersal of the Kurds*]. Dalawar Zanki (Trans.). Second Edition. Beirut: Amiral Print. 2011.

Benjamin H. Hary (1992). *Multiglossia in Judeo-Arabic.* Leiden, New York, Koln: E. J. Brill

Blochet, Edgard (1923). *Studies in The Pahlavi Grammar.* Pranabesh Sinha Roy (Trans.). The Static Society, Kolkata, 2005.

Bouckaert R, Lemey P, Dunn M, Greenhill SJ, Alekseyenko AV, Drummond AJ, Gray RD, Suchard MA, Atkinson QD. *Mapping the origins and expansion of the Indo-European language family.* Science. 2012 Aug 24;337(6097):957-60. doi: 10.1126/science.1219669. Erratum in: Science. 2013 Dec 20;342(6165):1446. PMID: 22923579; PMCID: PMC4112997.

Brown, H. D. (2007). *Principles of language learning and teaching.* (5th ed.). White Plains, NY: Pearson.

Chomsky, Noam (1965). *Aspects of the Theory of Syntax.* Massachusetts: The Massachusetts Institute Of Technology

Clyne, M. G. (1992). *Pluricentric Languages: Differing Norms in Different Nations.* Mouton de Gruyter. ISBN 9783110128550

Coulmas, Florian (2020). *Language and economy: Language industries in a Multilingual Europe.* Budapest: Hungarian Academy of Sciences.

Creet, Patrick Anthony Roger (1954). *Epistemology and Linguistics in the Philosophy of Thoma Hobbes.* University of British Columbia - Department of Philosophy and Psychology.

Cooper, Robert L.(1989). *Language planning and social change.* Cambridge: Cambridge University Press. ISBN 9780521333597.

De Saussure, Ferdinand (1959). *Course in General Linguistics.* New York: The Philosophical Library.

Everett, Daniel (2012). *Language the Cultural Tool.* London: Profile Books Ltd.

Ferguson, Charles A.(1959) *Sociolinguistic Perspectives: Pagers on Language in Society (Oxford Studies in Sociolinguistics).*

Fishman, Joshua A. (1967). *Bilingualism with and without Diglossia; Diglossia with and without Bilingualism.* Journal of Social Issues, 23, 29-38.

X. Unification

Fishman, Joshua A. (1991). *Reversing Language Shift: Theoretical and Empirical Foundations of Assistance to Threatened Languages.* Multilingual Matters.

Fossum, L. O. (1919). *A Practical Kurdish Grammar.* Minnesota: Augsburg Publishing House.

Frege, Gottlob (1919). Notes for Ludwig Darmstaedter. In M. Beaney (Ed.). (1979). *The Frege reader.* Oxford: Basil Blackwell. (Reprinted 2009).

Frohardt, Mark & Temin, Jonathan (Oct 2003). *Use and Abuse of Media in Vulnerable Societies.* New York: United States Institute of Peace (Special Report). <usip.org>

Garzoni, Maurizio (1787). *Grammatica e vocabolario della lingua Kurda.* Rome.

Gimbutas, Marija (1982). *The Goddesses and Gods of Old Europe 6500-3500 BC.* Berkeley, Los Angeles: University of California Press. Reprinted 1996

Hadank, Oskar Karl Mann (1932). *Mundarten der Zâzâ, hauptsächlich aus Siwerek und Kor [Dialects of the Zâzâ, mainly from Siwerek and Kor].* Berlin: Publishing house of the Prussian Academy of Sciences.

Halliday, M.A.K. (1978). *Language as Social Semiotic: The Social Interpretation of Language and Meaning.* University Park Press.

Howell, P. (Nov 2008). Effect of Speaking Environment on Speech Production and Perception. *J Hum Environ Syst.* 11(1):51-57. doi: 10.1618/jhes.11.51. PMID: 21258629; PMCID: PMC3024543.

<https://www.ncbi.nlm.nih.gov/pmc/articles/PMC3024543/#S18title>

Ibn Waḥshiyya (n.d). شوق المستهام في معرفة رموز الأقلام *[Epistemophile Longing to Lore Pen Codes].* Reprinted 2004.

Irvine, Judith. T. (1989). When Talk Isn't Cheap: Language and Political Economy. *American Ethnologist,* 16(2), 248–267. http://www.jstor.org/stable/645001

Kaplan, Robert B. & Baldauf, Richard B. (1997). *Language planning from practice to theory.* Clevedon: Multilingual Matters.

Keskin, Mesut (2017). *On the standardization efforts for a cross-dialectal literary language in Zazaki.* In Zeynep Arslan (Ed.). *Zazaki - yesterday, today and tomorrow: Survival and standardization of a threatened language.* Graz : Treffpunkt Sprachen, Forschungsbereich Plurilingualismus.

Kreyenbroek, Philip G. & Sperl, Stefan (2005). *The Kurds: A Contemporary Overview.* London: Routledge. ISBN 1134907656

Kustiawan W., Erwan Efendi H., Arfah K., Zul Akbar Shah, M. (Dec 2022). *Influence of mass media on social culture of communities.* Deliserdang, Indonesia: Infokum Journal. V 10. No 5. ISSN: 2302-9706. par 1, p 255. <infor.seaninstitute.org/index.php/infokum>

Laponce, Jean (2005). *La Gouvernance linguistique: Le Canada en perspective.* Ottawa: University of Ottawa. ISBN 9782760316225.

Leezenberg, Michiel (1993). *Gornai influence on central Kurdish: Substratum or prestige borrowing?* University of Amsterdam.

Lefebvre, Claire (1998). *Creole genesis and the acquisition of grammar.* Cambridge: Cambridge University Press.

Li, Chris Wen-Chao (2004) 'Conflicting notions of language purity: the interplay of archaising, ethnographic, reformist, elitist and xenophobic purism in the perception of Standard Chinese', Language & Communication. Volume 24. Issue 2. Pages 97-133. ISSN 0271-5309.

<https://doi.org/10.1016/j.langcom.2003.09.002>

Liu, Kang (Franco) (2018). *Chinese Speakers in America: Diglossia as Style,* Pomona College.

Lubotsky, Alexander (2020). "What language was spoken by the people of the Bactria-Margiana Archaeological Complex?", in Paul W. Kroll and Jonathan A. Silk (eds.), 'At the Shores of the Sky': Asian Studies for Albert Hoffstädt, Brill, Leiden/Boston

Lyons, John (1981). *Language and Linguistics.* Cambridge University Press. ISBN 978-0-521-29775-2.

MacKenzie D. N. (1971). *A Concise Pahlavi Dictionary.* Oxford University Press. (reprint 1986), ISBN 0 19 713559 5

X. Unification

Marschak, J. (1965): Economics of language. In: Behavioral Science 10 (2), 135-140

McArthur, Thomas Burns (1998). The English languages. Cambridge: Cambridge University Press.

McCarus, Ernest N. (1958). A Kurdish Grammar Descriptive and Analysis of the Kurdish of Sulaimaniya, Iraq. New York: American Council of Learned Societies.

McQuail, Denis (2010). McQuail's Mass Communication Theory (6th ed.). SAGE Publications Ltd.

Mkwinda-Nyasulu, Betty (2013). Role of language in socio-economic development: The semiotics are right. Journal of Humanities (23). ISSN: 1016-0728. pp 213-230

Naji, Ramzi. On the Origin and Causes of Sound Change: A Review of Related Literature (October 00, 2020). Sam Mohanlal, A. R. Fatihi, G. Baskaran, S. Chelliah, T. Deivasigamani, Pammi Pavan Kumar, Soibam Rebika Devi (eds.) Language in India. Vol. 19. India., Available at SSRN: <ssrn.com/abstract=3717891> or <dx.doi.org/10.2139/ssrn.3717891>

Nichols, Johanna (1998). The origin and dispersal of languages: Linguistic evidence. The Origin and Diversification of Language, pp. 127–70. (Memoirs of the California Academy of Sciences, 24.) San Francisco: California Academy of Sciences

Owens, Jonathan (Ed.). (2013). The Oxford Handbook of Arabic Linguistics. Oxford University Press. ISBN 978-0-19-976413-6

Parfitt, Tudor (1983) Ahad Ha-Am's Role in the Revival and Development of Hebrew. In: Kornberg, J., (ed.), At the crossroads: essays on Ahad Ha-am. New York: State University of New York Press, pp. 12–27.

Qamandar, Ismael (2014). دراسة لهجات الكردية الجنوبية [Study of southern Kurdish dialects]. Baghdad: Adnan Publishing.

Recasens, D. (1999). Lingual coarticulation. In W. J. Hardcastle & N. Hewlett (Eds). Cambridge: Cambridge University Press.

Renan, Ernest (1882). What is a Nation? (Qu'est-ce qu'une nation?). Ethan Rundell (Trans.) 1992. Paris: Presses-Pocket.

Russell, Aidan (2019). *Truth, Silence, and Violence in Emerging States: Histories of the Unspoken*. Milton, Oxfordshire: Routledge. ISBN 9781351141109

Russell, Bertrand (Oct 1905) On Denoting. *Mind*. Vol 14. No 56. p 490

Sapir, E. (1929). The Status of Linguistics as a Science. *Language*, 5(4), 207–214. https://doi.org/10.2307/409588

Schiffman, Harold F. (2003) *The Balance of Power in Multiglossic Languages: Implications for Language Shift*. EBSCO Publishing.

Silverstein, M. (1979). Language Structure and Linguistic Ideology. In P. Clyne, W. Hanks, and C. Hofbauer (Eds.), *The Elements* (pp. 193–248). Chicago: Chicago Linguistic Society.

Spengler, Oswald (1918). *The Decline of the West*. Charles F. Atkinson (Trans.). Oxford UP, 1991. ISBN 0-19-506751-7

Spolsky, Bernard (2004). *Language Policy*. Cambridge University Press.

Stark, Jaine P. (2010). *Kambari Orthography Design*. SIL International. ebook 16. ISBN 978-1-55671-245-6.

Steels, Luc & Szathmáry, Eörs. (2018) The evolutionary dynamics of language (Vol 164). *Biosystems*. ISSN 0303-2647. <https://doi.org/10.1016/j.biosystems.2017.11.003>

Sözeri, Fırat & konak, İsmet (2022). Dosya Kafkas Kürtlerı [File of Kurds in Caucasia]. *Kürt Araştırmaları Dergisi*. No 8. P51

Sweet, Henry (1899). *The Practical Study Of Languages*. London: J. M. Dent & Co.

Tam, Gina Anne. (2020) *Dialect and Nationalism in China, 1860–1960*. Cambridge University Press. ISBN 110847828X.

Thomas, George (1991). *Linguistic Purism*. Studies in Language and Linguistics. Longman. ISBN 9780582037427.

Todd, Terry Lynn; (2008). *A Grammar Of Dimili, Also Known As Zaza*. Electronic publication.

Wahbi, Tawfiq (Taufiq) (1956). قواعد اللغة الكردية [The Kurdish Grammar].
Baghdad

Weinreich, Uriel. 1968. Languages in Contact: Findings and Problems. The Hague: Mouton. [Originally published as Publications of the Linguistic Circle of New York, no. 1, 1953.]

Whorf, B. L. (1956). Language, Thought, and Reality: Selected Writings of Benjamin Lee Whorf. (John B. Carroll Ed.). New York, London: Massachusetts Institute of Technology & John Wiley & Sons, Inc., Reprinted 1959

Wittgenstein, Lodwig. (1922). Tractatus Logico-philosophicus.

Włodarczak, Marcin & Heldner, Mattias (2017). Respiratory Constraints in Verbal and Non-verbal Communication. Frontiers in Psychology. Vol 8.

<frontiersin.org/journals/psychology/articles/10.3389/fpsyg.2017.00708>

You, Yang. (2018). Language Unification, Labor and Ideology. Harvard University.

Yule, George (1985). The Study of Language, 4th Ed 2010; Cambridge: Cambridge University Press.

Yusupova, Zare A. (1998). Курдский диалект горани по литературным памятникам XVIII-XIX веков [The Kurdish dialect Gorani as represented in the literary monuments from 18th-19th cc.]. St. Petersburg, Nauka.

Yusupova, Zare A. (2017). The Kurdish Dialect Gorani: A Grammatical Description". Saarbrücken: Lambert Academic Publishing.

Zsiga, Elizabeth C. (2013). The sounds of language: an introduction to phonetics and phonology. Chichester, UK: Wiley-Blackwell. ISBN 978-1-4051-9103-6

www.ingramcontent.com/pod-product-compliance
Lightning Source LLC
Chambersburg PA
CBHW052138070526
44585CB00017B/1875